LOOK INSIDE
STOP SEEKING START LIVING

Michele Attias

R∃THINK PRESS

First published in Great Britain 2018
by Rethink Press (www.rethinkpress.com)

To my greatest expressions of self,
my daughters Jasmin and Olivia.

Praise

Look Inside is a compelling read, with short but perfectly formed chapters. Michele's book is humble, perceptive and heartfelt. She has what every great coach has: a huge heart and a passion to inspire. Job well done on all counts.

Michael Serwa – Coach For The Elite

Michele Attias has written a deeply personal and courageous book that I will be recommending far and wide. If you want to realign your life with success and well-being, get this book right now.

Steve Chandler – Author of *Time Warrior*

This book is a game changer! Through compelling personal and professional stories, Michele Attias artfully takes us on a journey of self-discovery and transformation. She leaves the reader with the tools and mindset necessary to help create lasting success in life. If you're ready to create an intentional and inspiring life, read this book now; your future self will thank you for it.

Devon Bandison – Coach and Author of *Fatherhood is Leadership: Your Playbook for Success, Self-Leadership and a Richer Life*

Michele's massive heart comes through in her words. Right from the start, my eyes were welling up. Her stories are as engaging as they are insightful. A great read for anyone wanting more out of life.

JP Morgan - Champion Coach

Relatable in a way that most books of this genre miss, Michele uses her own story to teach us how to leverage our inherent skill to create the life we want. The powerful lessons in this book are not preached at us as in many other books, but shared through story. This makes it not only a fascinating read, but relatable in a way that allows the reader to bring these lessons back into their own life.

David Schwendiman - Coach and Author of *Selling from the Top of the Ladder: the Ultimate Sales Playbook*

Michele Attias is an inspiring writer with an abundance of advice and guidance for leading and living fully and authentically. She provides beautiful examples of this throughout *Look Inside*, with stories from her own life and the lives of her clients. An uplifting and empowering book full of ideas on how each of us can evaluate the gifts we each have in us and what stops us from fully expressing them. A must read!

Sherry Welsh - Leadership Coach and Author of *Slowing Down*

Contents

CONTENTS

CONTENTS

Introduction

When you are born, you arrive blank, open, and game for whatever turns up. You then begin to base your truth on what you learn from others around you. This continues through to adulthood, and then we begin to look further outside ourselves to find that which was always safely tucked up within us.

People buy personal development books because they want someone to give them the skills and the secret formula for enjoying their lives more. They are seeking the answers from an outside source, rather than looking to their inner world, which is resourceful and limitless.

I was the biggest culprit in this respect for so many years, going on endless courses, online programmes, reading a multitude of books and travelling all around the world to find the magical pill that would make me complete and happy. What did I come back with? Nothing, except drained resources.

To my surprise, I found it at a time I least expected. I was emerging from a difficult personal experience, and I found that my external world as I knew it had evaporated. I had lost so much of what I believed had defined me for so many years. I realised that I had nothing else to cling to. It prompted me to go where

I had not gone before: through losing most of what I had, I found myself.

I found a wealth of resources inside me and a feeling of aliveness I had not experienced since my childhood. More importantly, what I began to create from that realisation was based on a mindset of having everything I needed already, instead of feeling as if I was missing something. My purpose is for you to find your own version of this.

We spend our lives living on the edge of what's possible, skirting around it, staring at what others are doing, looking for guidance, advice, even a guru who knows more than we do about our lives. It's always easier to look around at what others are doing than to carve our own path, but if I had settled into this mindset, you would not be holding my book right now.

I wrote this book whilst travelling on trains, buses, planes and ships to and through Thailand, Gibraltar, Spain, Morocco, Amsterdam, Israel, Chicago, New York, Nashville, Arizona, Paris and London, where I currently reside. We all have the potential to use our inner resources to create anywhere at any time, and use our insights to inform us what we need to do next. There is no perfect place or moment for this to happen.

Digging beneath the surface and teasing out our inner resilience and power takes courage, as we're often busy looking outside seeking the next thing that will give us a sense of belonging. I'm inviting you to build a degree of trust that you have everything you need already.

Just like the game at school, 'Show and Tell', which most of us loved to play, through my personal stories this book 'shows' you how to access more of the incredible resources that lie dormant within you, rather than 'tells' you what you need to do next.

Stop the search and start living through (not outside) your unique and powerful self.

Part One
REACHING OUT

1: Empowerment Through Inspiration

Words have an incredible power to destroy or rebuild a person.

Let's backtrack. The year was 1971. A teacher at my primary school announced to me one day, 'You will never make anything of yourself.'.

I was aged four at the time, and whilst I heard her words, I didn't really comprehend the enormity of what she had just said. I wonder if any of the kids in the class remembered a thing she taught that day (or the whole year, for that matter) other than the ill-advised words aimed at me.

The next day, my father stormed into the school office to complain about the teacher's comment, but it was too late. The damage had been done.

During the next few years, if I answered any maths questions incorrectly (maths was my weakest subject), one of the teachers would take me out of the class and walk me down to the lower form classes. She would then inform the younger students of my mistakes, whilst I stood at the front of the class, feeling the sense of shame that comes from knowing you have failed at something huge, yet not knowing why such a fuss is being made over an incorrect maths equation.

Is it any wonder that by the time I left primary school at the age of 13, high school had become my nirvana?

High school was a convent school (apparently haunted) run by a group of Irish nuns. The concept of this seemed unbelievable to me at the time. As a Jewish girl at a convent school, I entered adolescence with a thick mixture of two very different religions, but as we lived in an area which spanned two and a half square miles in the south of Spain, and there were no other high schools, it was take it or leave it. And we couldn't afford to leave it.

In the unfamiliar arena of Holy Communion, Confession and the Lord's Prayer – all so different to the traditions that my community followed – I woke up and smelt the coffee. Or rather, the pungent smells of burning incense. The nuns' Irish accents were in stark contrast to the children's loud Spanish voices which permeated the air. I wondered what the nuns made of hormonal adolescent girls displaying a mix of passionate Span-ish blood amongst the traditional Roman Catholic structure and politeness.

At high school I was tenacious, impulsive – and lived for my dance and drama lessons. In addition, I had a number of boy-friends and a busy social life. I was at the centre of the friendship circles and totally belonged.

There was only one problem, and it was huge.

1: EMPOWERMENT THROUGH INSPIRATION

After my early years of being manhandled and given a number of colourful put downs by teachers, I had no faith or belief whatsoever in my academic ability. I spent my time playing around in class, holding no aspirations for advancement. The concept of attending university was so alien to me, I had not even allowed it to filter through. In my mind, academic achievement was reserved for an exclusive circle of VIPs, which certainly did not include me. I had no desire to reach for anything other than perhaps a dance, beauty or hairdressing course. I secretly aspired to become a dancer, yet this was forbidden from the outset, as my parents decided it would never provide a secure enough living.

There was one exception, though – Sister Anne's English class. The only class I dared to take an interest in.

Even though my spoken English was pretty basic, I didn't struggle at all to write stories, effortlessly allowing my mind and imagination to run riot. On paper I was free to create the beginning and dream ending I wanted, all with the free flow of an artist painting a masterpiece.

Other than dancing, my only saving grace was reading. I was never happier than when I was settling down with a new book, and I remember running after school on Fridays to our local curiosity shop, which was a tiny bookshop selling second-hand English books. I loved the smell and feel of the paper as I turned the pages. Fitting my reading into the weekend between parties and socials, I would proceed to devour books one by one whilst I snuggled up on the sofa. The books transported me to a world where I could be the VIP in a way I could never be in the school academic circle.

It is not really a surprise, therefore, that my inspirational moment came in Sister Anne's English class. How did this Irish nun change my life? She woke me up to what I was capable of.

Sister Anne sat me down one day when I had been particularly raucous in the classroom and told me sternly that she would have to call my parents for a serious discussion. This of course filled me with deep shame and embarrassment. Snapshots of my past failures in primary school came back to haunt me.

Sister Anne said, 'Mee-chele,' (her Irish pronunciation changed the spelling of my name) 'you're wasting your life. Do you always want to be the class clown?'

Her next statement was the winning formula.

'I want you to take the advanced English exam, because I know you can do well. You're a clever girl; I want you to start working hard. Aim high, because you are so capable.'

No one in the teaching profession had ever mentioned the word 'capable' in relation to me before. My parents had implied that I was capable, but I figured that parents had to say that, even if their children were as thick as two planks. But here's the deal – it wasn't just the words that Sister Anne fired at me with the precision of a well-aimed arrow; it was the manner in which they were delivered: with care and love. She could see my potential before

I had even woken up to it. Here was a teacher who actually did what it says on the tin: teach, inspire and empower.

Words and the intention behind them are incredibly powerful and can make or break a person. From that day, I stopped behaving like the class clown and focused on my studies. By the end of the year, I was receiving top marks – a concept that would have been completely inconceivable before. I had always been capable; I just needed someone to tell me that I was. It was as simple as that.

Many years later, after I qualified as a therapist, my first job was managing therapy services for children in primary schools. It was almost as if I had gone back in time and had the opportunity to give kids the type of positive and empowering atmosphere in primary school that I hadn't had the chance to experience. For many years, I listened, empathised with, empowered and nurtured children who came from so many diverse backgrounds. Many of them were refugees from war-torn countries, all displaced and confused in a melee of 120 languages and spanning so many cultures from all over the world. I have listened to children pleading for attention, security, understanding and love, their backgrounds spanning the social and economic sector: wealthy, poor, neglected, abused, abandoned, fostered or adopted. Along the way, I have always felt like I had Sister Anne by my side, looking at me with her sidelong glance.

It is the simple act of showing humanity and sharing humility with another person by waking them up to what you see in them, in the hope that they will start seeing it within themselves.

If we deduct religion, culture and language, and we take it down to its very core, I believe there is one thing we all yearn for. Love; it's as simple as that. When the Beatles sang 'All you need is love,' they were spot on.

The beauty of what Sister Anne, the Irish nun, taught me was that having love for another human being, and empathy, spans across every sector of humanity. She had her strong Catholic beliefs whilst, as a Jewish teen, I had my strong own beliefs and traditions. Yet we were able to dissolve what could have divided us and discover a deeper connection that inspired me enough to empower and believe in the potential of others.

I can still see the lovely Sister Anne in my mind, her radiant face glowing as she stood with her glasses sliding slowly down her nose, observing my progress. This is the look I pass on to my coaching clients as I watch them transform into better versions of themselves.

The reality is that we can all be a hero in someone's life by showing them a quality in themselves that money can't buy. There is a Sister Anne in each and every one of us, and it only takes a moment to connect with someone. That person could be a friend, neighbour, colleague, elderly person living in isolation, or child desperately seeking attention.

Reach out to them and be that inspiration.

2: Find Your Inner Superhero

A lady fainted at 8.30am in a packed train carriage one morning. No one looked up or paid the slightest bit of notice. Around me, I observed a woman staring at her phone, a man reading the Bible (ironic given the circumstances), and a variety of people reading the *Metro* newspaper. None of them seemed interested enough to extract themselves from their mindless tasks and observe what was going on in front of them.

The lady who fainted had been keeling over for a few minutes, white as a sheet and visibly sweating. She was breathing heavily, and then proceeded to take her jacket off.

I spoke. I asked everyone in my carriage, 'Do you know if this lady is okay? She looks pretty unwell!'

Still most people stayed glued to their phones or books. They seemed reluctant to respond, as this could mean being sucked into (dare I say it?) helping, or what they might call a 'situation'. The gentleman sitting next to her looked nervously around the train carriage. I could see in his face he was hoping and praying that someone else would take responsibility for her; he certainly didn't want to.

I was sitting opposite the fainting lady and prodded her arm.

'Are you okay?' I asked.

'No, I'm not,' she grumbled weakly.

Still, everybody pretended not to hear. I spoke to the passengers again.

'Let's get some help at the next station. Does anyone have any water we can give her?'

Again, they stayed glued to their seats. Anyone would have thought I was asking them to part with a wad of cash.

During this 8.30am trip into the City, I encountered a resistance to helping, to simply reaching out and connecting. This resistance has become disturbingly prevalent in our society.

I believe the reason people consume endless products and have endless relationships is that they want to feel connected. They want to feel something – anything. Yet here was a woman clearly unwell on the train and no one bothered to care and extend their hand, even though the feeling they would have got from helping would have been far more rewarding than staring at their phones.

It's no wonder we have the Pride of Britain event each year, where anyone who has done something special is given a much-deserved award. These people have reached out and done what others wouldn't. Importantly, they cared, put themselves out and valued others before themselves.

What if we could be that kind of hero every day? The person who reaches out when someone trips on the street, chats to a lonely person sitting in a café, or helps a woman who is fainting on a packed morning train. What if, as a society, we stopped being so suspicious of others' motives and simply connected, loved, supported and gave something back, rather than expecting others to do it? What if we could show up in life like Superman, Batman, Wonder Woman, or whichever superhero we worshipped as children? Imagine how much more connected we would feel as we went about our everyday life.

Instead of expecting politicians to change your world, be the change you want to see, even in the smallest of ways. A 5% increase in how responsive you are to your surroundings could make a huge impact. It might start with supporting someone you see struggling as you go about your everyday life, and it could extend to changing someone's life.

There is no more powerful feeling than this.

3: Observe What's Around You

It all started with a bacon sandwich. Not my own, I'm afraid – being Jewish doesn't allow me to indulge in such a delicacy.

The bacon sandwich was requested by a homeless man outside a busy Pret a Manger café in the heart of London. Business-people lined the early morning streets, all looking important and accomplished, rushing in their haste to create the next app, develop a new program, or innovate in ways we can only dream of. Yet in the midst of this busyness sat a man on the pavement with a blanket over his legs. It was a cold morning and he was shivering, but no one bothered to take a second look. I wondered if this guy had morphed into a computer, iPad or iPhone whether they would have paid him more attention.

As I walked past, I couldn't resist asking him if I could get him a sandwich or a breakfast roll. He looked at me, and his eyes lit up. Finally he had been noticed and acknowledged.

I took a moment to reflect on how he could have ended up in this state. Surely if any one of us was down on our luck, we would have relatives who would put us up, give us a place to sleep or a bowl of hot soup? I'm always curious to know how someone can start off as a member of society and end up on the streets asking for spare change, looking as if a simple wash would be their best next step.

The homeless man asked me if I could buy him a sandwich. Not just any sandwich, but a bacon sandwich. He knew exactly where it was in Pret a Manger since he could see it in the large display window across from where he sat outside. The food was all visible to him. So near and yet so far! He asked if he could have it heated up and licked his lips at the prospect of tucking in.

I bought him the sandwich and asked, 'Are you Irish?'

A smile transformed his features. As he spoke to me about how he had arrived from Ireland a few years ago, he suddenly did something that took my breath away. In fact, it brought tears to my eyes.

He lifted the blanket that was draped over his legs to reveal a large dog cuddling up to him. This had previously not been visible to me at all.

The man explained with sadness that the night before, the police had threatened to take the dog away, and he had pleaded with them to let him keep his dog. It was clear to me that the dog was clinging on to this man for dear life. Interestingly enough, the dog regarded his owner as a source of security and comfort, even though they had nowhere to live, nor any prospects to speak of.

The man continued, 'I need to sort myself out for my dog's sake. She needs me. I have to find a place to live – I must do it.'

Talk about a clear purpose.

This encounter reminded me of the number of times I had wrestled with whether to rehome my dog due to unnecessary anxiety about the future. Yet here was a man showing me the true meaning of commitment. Not a wishy-washy version dependent on external factors, but an unconditional commitment to what was important to him. Imagine if he transferred that commitment to holding down a job, finding a place to live, and rebuilding his life. We can learn so much from that moment.

Watching the tenderness he showed towards his dog brought tears to my eyes.

I observed as the busyness in the street increased, yet people were missing what was right in front of their noses. They were missing the beauty of humanity: the care, love and affection that everyone can feel for another being. I doubt any of the City high-flyers could have measured up to the deep intention that this guy had demonstrated.

We need to open our eyes more, look at the world and see beyond what is presented to us. Failing to do this, we run the risk of living a half-life, missing what is around us every day. Reach out, speak to others, connect and care as if your life depends on it. Because it does.

4: Communicating and Connecting

Ever since we learnt to speak, many of us will have been told not to talk to strangers. Whilst this might have been totally appropriate when we were toddlers, sometimes we continue to observe this as we transition into adulthood.

According to *Scientific American*, it has been proven that people are happier after talking to strangers, even if they thought beforehand that they would detest it. I experienced this for myself a while back when I entered a packed bus in the early morning rush hour. As I sat down, I noticed a man sitting across from me, sobbing uncontrollably. He was holding a bottle of beer as if his life depended on it. The people around him were watching in the same way they would watch a television programme you can switch off at any moment as he continued to sob and wail, using his worn sleeve as a substitute tissue to wipe his nose, which was becoming as red as his teary eyes.

My challenges here were twofold. Not only was he sitting in a place I could not ignore, but as I am a coach and was previously a therapist, a distressed man to me was like waving a juicy prime cut of beef at a hungry lion.

I nudged the lady next to me and asked, 'Have you checked if he's okay?'

She responded, 'Ignore him; he's probably drunk.'

Of course I couldn't leave it.

'What's wrong?' My question punctured the air.

'Do you know where I've come from?' he replied as he wiped his eyes. 'I've just came out of jail where I spent the night, because my schizophrenic girlfriend made an accusation against me. The thing is, I suffer from depression. She has three children, I've got children of my own, and she is currently pregnant with my baby.'

He burst into tears again, whilst I sat there with my mouth wide open in shock. This was the reason behind the 'drunkard' weeping on the bus.

He took another sip from his bottle like a baby wanting comfort from his milk.

'Does the beer help you?' I asked.

'Yes, it does,' he replied.

'Where are the children?'

'At home. I'm going to see them now and I will tell them that I'm leaving them. I have to, even though I love them as if they were my own.'

I could feel his heartbreak at having to say goodbye to these young beings he adored, but he simply couldn't endure staying with a partner who was highly dysfunctional. Such was the dilemma he was facing, and so tears of loss were pouring out of him. He was deeply scared, emotional and confused.

After speaking continuously giving even more details about the saga, his expression suddenly changed and he looked enlightened.

'You know,' he said, 'talking to you has made me feel so much better. I feel happier.'

With this comment he stood up, blessed me and stepped gingerly out of the bus and back into his dysfunctional life, whilst I continued the journey into mine.

I'm not downplaying my coaching skills, but I did not coach this man. My only comments were 'I'm sorry to hear that' and 'This must be so hard for you to deal with', and I nodded every so often whilst truly empathising with him. It reminded me of bestselling author and coach Michael Neill's remarkable wisdom: 'If all you did was tell a lamppost your goals for each day, they would still be far more likely to happen.'

As I peeled through the layers of his story, I realised he was publicly expressing his sadness, waiting for someone to ask him if he was okay. He needed to receive validation and understanding, despite the fact that he might be dismissed as a drunkard with no job, prospects or money.

In the culture I grew up in, in the south of Spain, if people were experiencing overwhelming problems they'd hop on to a bus or walk through the cobbled streets and share their story with the first person who greeted them. All that person needed to do was nod every so often and show understanding. By the time they had reached their destination, they'd feel as light as a feather.

Often all we require is to feel acknowledged. If someone listens to our experience, lending a sympathetic ear to our story, our thinking shifts. The problems no longer feel so overwhelming and become more manageable. Then insights and wisdom which point us in the right direction can push through. Our thoughts clear like an overcast sky, and it is then possible to experience the beautiful starry night behind them.

5: A Coffee Can Change the World

Who could have imagined that offering a homeless lady a cup of coffee would change my day?

Navigating through my professional life, I was recently fortunate enough to come across a Kindness CEO for a charity promoting random acts of kindness through buying a cup of coffee for someone who actually needs it. The act is more than just buying a coffee, though; it provides conversation, comfort, a smile, even a laugh. Currently, over 2,000 cafés around the world have engaged in this project, and have an online presence of over 30,000 subscribers. This project has touched and changed the lives of millions of disadvantaged people.

Their mission is to bring communities together in hope, and to inspire and empower others to change lives and restore our faith in humanity. They have also added another strand to their mission statement: 'Be kind to others, but be kind to yourself, too.'

After connecting with this organisation at an event recently, I was feeling tremendously inspired. As I travelled back to London, I came across a lady sitting on the ground, which was littered with cast-aside newspapers. Her face was tear-stained and her expression was one of intense despair. Normally, I would have given her some money, a smile of greeting, and walked off. But inspired by John's message of kindness, I asked her if she wanted a hot drink.

She looked at me, obviously barely able to believe I was engaging her in conversation, then nodded her head and requested a coffee. I ran down to the coffee shop in the station to fetch her drink. As I returned, I noticed her hands were dirty, her shoes were torn, and the few possessions she had left were bundled up in a tattered old bag.

Deciding to ignore her physical appearance, I sat next to her. I asked her why she had been crying earlier and she looked up at me, appearing to be even more shocked than she had been before. It was clear that she was neither used to nor expecting any attention. As she sat on the filthy ground outside the station, she might have imagined she didn't matter; that no one cared. But here's the thing: she did matter.

As we sat there – me in my high-end work wear and her in an assortment of materials wrapped around her – we were simply two human beings connecting and engaging in conversation. What separated us were people's judgements and preconceived ideas about how we each presented ourselves to the world. To the general public, she was simply a faceless homeless person, and to a homeless person, I was a faceless stranger who had a more fortunate set of circumstances.

If we bother to scratch beneath the surface, we all have the ability to feel pain, loss, anxiety, confusion and resentment.

Status and financial standing doesn't protect us from this. We are all the same; we just need to stop dividing ourselves and start connecting more.

We spoke for a while and I listened to her story, which was punctuated with tears of desperation. Our conversation helped her to shift her mindset, and a ray of hope entered it. By the time I bid her farewell and stood up to leave, I felt something monumental had changed inside me.

Forget about the cup of coffee and conversation I provided for this lady; she woke me up by allowing her vulnerability to be raw and exposed. It's actually rare that we see vulnerability exhibited nowadays. Many people spend their lives either pretending all is well, or trying to keep it together so that no one will ever see their defences collapse. How refreshing it was to meet someone who could show me their struggles and pain without anything getting in the way. It reminded me of how each of us has the potential to make a difference (however small) one person at a time.

We don't need to be the next celebrity or member of the elite to make a change. It all starts with the small things: an act of kindness; friendly eye contact; care; and giving. They all have the potential to impact others.

What small act of kindness could you do today?

6: Deepening Your Relationships

Relationships can feel like a conundrum, but we do need to give thought to their quality and depth.

Every relationship is different, and we could get caught up in thinking we need to be different in each one. But what if our bonds with parents, children, spouse, siblings and business colleagues could all have the same consistency, depth, understanding, love and connection? It's achievable if we focus our energies on what we want to create.

Ask yourself, 'What do I need to create a great relationship?' How about adding an element of curiosity?

Have you heard the popular old proverb 'Curiosity killed the cat'? It warns us of the dangers of unnecessary investigation, and I remember having it drummed into my mind as I ventured out as child. I was forever exploring due to being curious enough to go the extra mile to discover something tempting. In my early years I wanted to become an archaeologist and travel to Egypt to discover and dig up enchanting treasures. I had no idea how valuable this curiosity would be later on in my life, particularly when I went on to create my coaching business. It has no doubt shaped my relationships with my clients. Instead of digging up treasures in Egypt, I dig deep to find my clients' hidden treasures.

Essentially, curiosity in a relationship invites questions, and this requires you to become something of a Sherlock Holmes. The results when you incorporate curiosity into your interactions and relationships are likely to astound you.

For example, ask your child how their day was. Their answer will possibly range from 'boring' to 'fantastic'. If your tendency is to leave that conversation where it is and move on, do something different. How about asking a further question? Why was it boring/fantastic/good? What precisely made it so? And so on. This is a great way of shaping your relationship because you're showing you're actually interested in how their day was.

Interaction with the people around you is even better if you're asking questions without holding a mobile phone or in the midst of sending an e-mail. Be more present. This shift made a huge difference in my relationship with family, friends and whilst networking.

People love to be asked about themselves. Taking an interest can add a new dimension to the conversation and, ultimately, the relationship. Asking the question underneath the question might uncover more than you realised. The person you're talking to will feel acknowledged, understood and valued because you're taking time to listen to them. You can reshape and re-craft the quality of your relationships simply by making small shifts and tweaks.

A few years ago, at a leadership workshop, I became acquainted with a man whom I recognised from a YouTube video. I couldn't articulate why, but I instantly felt connected to him, despite the fact that he barely spoke at the workshop. I decided to contact him via e-mail. In response to my e-mail, he was curious enough to ask why I had chosen to connect with him.

In a vague sort of way, I described why I had been drawn to the vision he had presented at the workshop. He responded with a second e-mail which stipulated that this was not enough for him to go on. He didn't feel connected to my reason for making contact, and asked that I gave him more details. At his request, I went deeper and sent him a pretty long e-mail.

His next correspondence stated that he wanted a conversation with me and we set up a Skype session. Since we had already created a platform from which to develop our relationship, the Skype session was truly incredible. In fact, I hired him there and then to work with me.

This taught me a lesson in leading through curiosity by digging deep and requesting more information. It is a great model for creating meaningful relationships. We have a choice to create a platform which is either shallow and superficial, or meaningful and memorable.

7: Pursue Service

When reflecting on the impact we can have on another person, I think back to a year ago when a tiny mosquito bit the side of my right leg, causing it to triple in size. The ripple effects of this were intense. They involved cancelling travel plans and rearranging my life with military precision.

If an insignificant mosquito was capable of changing my life, imagine the impact a person could have. This is absolutely crucial to remember when we're approaching life with a service mindset.

So what does service mean exactly? Being of service to someone means we have chosen to engage and fulfil by giving unconditionally. We don't need to derive happiness from the other person's reaction to our service, because we are already good to go. The mere act of being of service makes us happy. But this doesn't mean we become martyrs to the cause or make undue sacrifices that have an emotional, physical, spiritual or financial cost.

Most of us started our careers wanting to make a difference; we sought to be of service to others. As time went by, we began to question and measure our worth, perhaps even comparing what we were doing with others in our field. Meanwhile, the service we gave to our clients sailed further away into the sunset.

It's as if we have been given a magic wand capable of touching someone's life and transforming it immeasurably. So we focus on the wand. Is it the right colour and style? Might it need a polish? Is it as big and glitzy as other wands? Perhaps it should look different.

This renders us incapable of reaching out. By the time the comparison and self-worth game has ended, it is too late to serve someone who might have been in need. We hesitate and proceed through mountains of anxious overthinking about who we need to be before serving.

Even when each barrier is broken, serving can often feel heavy with expectation. If we serve someone and there's a positive response, it's a success story. Yet if there's no response, it's marked by failure. We then dare not venture out on to that platform again. There is a tangible tension between service and expectation.

But what if we could reach out and serve by letting go of the result?

I believe we need to approach service with humility and a fearless heart. It's so rare these days to receive true service through a written note, a personal e-mail or a book through the post. But when someone does this, we never forget them.

It's challenging to serve someone if you're holding on to expectations. Let go of impressing and simply express through an authentic desire to help. The only question we need to ask is 'How can I serve this person?' Imagine, in addition to sending out e-mail marketing or newsletters to our subscribers each week, if we focused on serving just a handful of our customers deeply with a personal e-mail or handwritten note. Offer something unique. No one wants to be treated like a number within a marketing system; people want to be noticed, acknowledged and understood. The only thing that matters is to keep the other person in mind. Take yourself out of the equation and give without fear.

Dale Carnegie put it beautifully when he said, 'Do things for others and you'll find your self-consciousness evaporating like morning dew.'

I remember almost 20 years ago, as a single parent with two very young children, I wondered how I would continue to work, grow as a professional, run a home and raise my children successfully. I was no Mary Poppins, so I decided that if it was all going to function, I needed to find a system that made no-one feel demoralised or ignored within the family, including myself as a parent. Certainly this is not easy to achieve when you're bringing up children on your own!

I created a system called the 'Special Day'. This allowed each of us to have our own day of the week (mine was Monday). Even my cleaner got a Special Day which she found amusing, but she also mattered. I never wanted anyone to feel as if I was taking them for granted.

When the Special Day arrived, the person whose day it was would be treated as a VIP the entire day. Everyone loved it and felt excited as their day approached. There was no need for attention-seeking behaviour (including from me), childish tantrums or hissy fits, as everyone had the opportunity to feel special. To this day, my grown up daughters recall this with fondness.

What if you served your clients in the same way? Each day, choose a client or prospect you would like to reach out to – just one client. Treat them to a phone call, an article you've read that might amuse them or an audio that could really help them with something they're dealing with. If you've connected with them before, you will know what's important to them and what they value. Send that person something which shows they matter to you. This makes the client feel noticed, acknowledged and special. More importantly, you will be doing something that sets you and your business apart. You're not contacting them alongside thousands of other people; you're connecting to create a personal relationship which will grow and show them you care. They are no longer a number on your list, but have been promoted to the status of human being.

A few months ago, I was coaching a business Manager who was attending a business event and wanted to engage with a number of companies whilst he was there. He shared that he had always been highly unsuccessful when approaching companies at events.

I encouraged him to do something different. I asked him to think of three companies he wanted to approach and focus only on how he would serve them. He was to research everything he needed to know about the companies and their teams, spending a few hours each week on this, reading through their website content and thinking of how he could add value to their business. He would then know them intimately before he had even engaged them in conversation.

To my delight, over the next few weeks, he diligently spent time slowing the process right down and preparing ahead, focusing on how he could best serve the companies he'd chosen with his level of expertise. He began to enjoy the change he was experiencing within himself and even felt more committed to attending.

On the day of the event, I curiously wondered how it had gone. He contacted me in the middle of the afternoon, more excited than I had ever heard him before. Not only had the contacts he'd spent weeks nurturing engaged with him, but there was now a queue of people waiting to speak to him. The whole process had created within him a deeper intention and a sense of purpose.

The key here is that he wasn't focused on selling, he was focused on serving. He took his ego out of the equation, stopped impressing and simply focused on helping, wanting to give something back. No wonder he attracted people around him like bees to a honeypot.

A big part of the process of service without expectation is letting go of fear. Replace 'Who am I to serve?' with 'How could I best be of service?' If you suspend fear and let go of the outcome, you give without holding back. It's not easy and requires diligent practice, but the benefits are massive. The person you serve may or may not become your client, but I can assure you they will remember you and may well recommend you to others, because in these days of automated systems, so few people are actually reaching out in this way.

Play with reaching out to someone and letting go of the outcome. Observe what this feels like. Fearless giving is freeing in a way that can't be imagined – it can only be experienced.

Those you reach out to owe you nothing. If you invest in the relationship by serving, then you do so with goodwill. Giving a focused hour each day or week to serving is not a huge investment of time. It certainly beats spending that same hour hounding prospects on social media platforms. Like planting seeds, the service we give grows and bears incredibly juicy fruit. It requires trust in yourself, so don't hold back. Pursue fearless giving.

8: Focus on Connection

One of the best and most poignant speeches I have ever heard was from a Slovakian who, in broken English, spoke about his journey into entrepreneurship. He had been invited to speak at a conference full of the bigwigs of the start-up world and stood up on stage, admitting to everyone how anxious he was feeling. The speakers amongst the audience (myself included) breathed a sigh of relief; we were not alone. He pulled at our heart strings without using any type of manipulation or self-healing, and came across more genuine than anyone who had prepared a perfect PowerPoint presentation.

He was the only speaker who stayed in my mind after the conference was over. His message came across loud and clear in a seemingly effortless manner. It was far from polished, but the authenticity he radiated was palpable, and this was what made him so unique and memorable. He had built a successful business, but he didn't focus on patting himself on the back. Instead, he spoke about his elderly grandfather who had inspired him in his darkest moments. You could have heard a pin drop in the silence that reigned throughout his speech.

This made me reflect on how far we go to create the perfect image, speech or website, all the while missing the one essential factor:

emotional connection to those we are meant to be serving. This doesn't mean that we should show up at an event badly prepared or unprofessional in our demeanour; it just means not trying to impress, building relationships and connection instead.

As a coach, I have had clients whose biggest fear is that they will be 'found out'. Not for an extra-marital affair, murder or burglary, but for being imperfect and not having the answer to every question. It is a real fear, like an addiction which demands attention when it's not being fed. I observe this more often with those in the corporate world: an often predatory world where 'vulnerability' is almost a dirty word. It never surprises me to see a bunch of corporate employees pacing outside the impressive buildings of Canary Wharf in London, smoking cigarettes before 9am. I can only imagine the stress they are under, not only to complete a hard day's work, but to do so in a way that doesn't allow for imperfection or flaws to seep in – or worse, expose them as incompetent.

It is hard to drop preconceived ideas of what we believe others need from us.

What would happen if you called yourself out on your imperfections? Imagine if you could be more fluid, less measured, more informal, and say, 'I don't know,' more often, allowing others to see you as human. What would this do to your stress levels?

This doesn't mean turning yourself into a buffoon who can't or won't answer a question. But there are times when we really don't know; when we are in the midst of uncertainty; when we have to develop the curiosity of a child to understand what is occurring.

It's not by chance that the know-it-alls at school were often the more unpopular kids. Who could connect with a so-called 'perfect' kid when we were all struggling to attain decent grades?

A client was concerned about attending a conference that could gain him some great connections and clients. His focus was on his credentials looking good. He felt he needed to look polished and let others know what he could offer them.

He had never been successful at conferences; he tended to overthink and place strategy before human connection. Yet he expected business to be magically attracted by this ineffective combination. I could totally identify with him behaving in this way.

I reminded him that he needed to focus on expressing, not impressing; by being present in the conversation his body language would be a clear indicator of this. To allow others to become familiar with him on a human level.

The question everyone wants to ask when they meet you is 'Can you help me?' not 'How perfect are you?' I have been coached and mentored by flawed and imperfect beings who at times got it wrong, but their care and connection to their purpose was clear. This is what matters to me.

There is relief in my clients' faces when I tell them that sometimes I don't know the answer to their question. I am not perfect, and I certainly have not always made great decisions or led a blissful life in the past. Essentially, I'm not required to be perfect in order to facilitate someone's journey into success. I simply need to listen, ask questions, be authentic, call myself out when I get it wrong, and accompany clients to where they want to go with love and care. This demonstrates an important and often life-changing lesson to my clients: they can be vulnerable and imperfect too. They don't need to pretend to be perfect, because I simply don't care for perfection. Instead, I'm just seeking their truth so that we can build on that foundation.

The mistake that many of us make is to try to impress those we desperately want to connect with. This creates barriers and little else. When we are viewed as flawed, imperfect, vulnerable and real, it allows others to drop their defences and relate to us on a totally different level. This doesn't mean professionalism is thrown out of the window. We can still keep boundaries, yet show humanity and connection within them.

To be human is to err, endeavour to forgive and release judgement. Perhaps in the Victorian era, when people had to keep a stiff upper lip and pretend all was well, being judgmental might have worked. Currently, people want to feel an emotional connection to you both in a personal and professional setting. They want to feel something that goes beyond a slick website or promotional material. If you can provide them with this, you will be memorable, not because you're forcing an impression, but because you're removing what's getting in the way of accessing their humanity.

Part Two
INNER STRENGTH

9: Resilience in the Face of Adversity

I t's a scenario many people dread: the moment a stranger enters your car and drives off – with you inside it.

This happened to me in the summer of 1996. It was a warm afternoon with a slight breeze, and no warning of what was about to happen. It didn't occur in an inner-city back street or alleyway, but in a bustling street, jam-packed with people doing their weekend shopping.

That afternoon, my husband (soon to be ex-husband) left the car whilst I sat in the passenger seat, observing the general vibe and atmosphere around me. I had recently become a first-time mum to a beautiful baby daughter, and I was reflecting on all the changes that had occurred since her birth. In the middle of my quiet contentment, I couldn't have been more unprepared for what was about to take place.

The driver's side door opened and in stepped a man I didn't recognise. He was a young guy with cropped blond hair. In my naïveté, I turned to him and pointed out that he seemed to have got into the wrong car.

He looked at me coldly and said, 'I'm in the right car.'

With that, he forced the key into the ignition and drove off whilst I stared at him in disbelief. I should have screamed, panicked, fainted, but here's the thing – I was as cool as a cucumber. I feel more anxiety when I receive a tax bill in the post, when my accountant sends me an email, or when I reach my car and find yet another parking ticket with another hefty fine to pay. Yet here I was being carjacked, and I was as relaxed and nonchalant as could be.

THE BODY HAS AN INCREDIBLE INTELLIGENCE SYSTEM. This coping mechanism cuts itself off from sensation during times of danger. Imagine an electrical circuit. When there's an overload of electricity, the system just shuts down. In the human body, this shutting down protects you from feeling too much or being too overwhelmed, resulting in more clarity.

TRUST YOUR WISDOM AND GUT FEELING. Throughout the whole process, I had a gut feeling, even trust, that all would be well. I did not allow myself for one second to become consumed with thinking of worse-case scenarios. I simply resigned myself to what was happening and let each moment dictate what needed to happen next, effortlessly developing a focus I didn't even know I possessed.

ACCESS THE HUMANITY OF THE OTHER PERSON IF POS-SIBLE. The first thing I did when the guy drove off with me inside the car was to engage him in conversation. To illustrate the extent of this conversation, I actually laughed as I told him that the last thing I imagined doing on a Sunday afternoon was being taken for a drive by a stranger. If I could ensure he connected with me as a human being, he might then not want to inflict any pain on me. Bizarre though it seems, my gut feeling led with this option and I followed obligingly.

To my utter amazement (and confusion), the guy drove around the area without uttering a word in response to my invitation to engage in conversation. He then turned right, back to the road he had picked me up from, and parked in exactly the same spot we had started from. In a swift movement, he stepped out of my car.

I never saw him again.

As I sat glued to my seat, imagining I had been in some kind of warped dream, my husband climbed back into the car. He was totally oblivious to what had transpired during the 30 minutes he had spent shopping. His world had stayed the same, but mine hadn't. Nothing ever looked the same again.

As the hours ticked on, my system began to wake up to the reality of what had occurred. In waking up from my trance, I reflected on my role as a wife and mother who could have disappeared from the planet. Who knows where this guy could have taken me and if I would have survived? What would have happened to my baby girl if I hadn't survived? I would have missed the beautiful years of her life.

None of this had been at the forefront of my mind as the guy had driven off with me a few hours earlier.

When I hear 'post-traumatic stress disorder' mentioned, I imagine this is what I experienced psychologically. However, it isn't a disorder; just the opposite. Our internal system is an extremely intelligent one which closes off when traumatic experiences occur so that we can manage what we need to do in the moment to keep us safe. Once the body is no longer in survival mode, it relaxes, and the feelings which return like a tidal wave are often overwhelming and difficult to manage. This is what is experienced as trauma, but it's actually the natural aftermath of a traumatic experience.

As I stand here many years on, my daughters (yes, I added a second daughter to my already busy routine) are aware of my obsession with always locking the door the moment I enter the car. A small price to pay to avoid a repetition of an experience that could have been monumentally worse. Just like the internal locking mechanism of the car, my own internal system locks up unhelpful thinking. And this keeps me safe, resilient and ready to face life.

10: Find Your Voice

Some time ago, I found myself in the midst of decision making (not my favourite pursuit) and all that happens when others don't share my views – in fact, in the thick of all the changes that take place within us when we face opposition.

John Demartini, one of the world's leading authorities on human behaviour and personal development, stated, 'When the voice and the vision on the inside is more profound, and more clear and loud than all the opinions on the outside, you've begun to master your life.' This immediately resonated with me and made an enormous amount of sense, yet it was so incredibly difficult to execute.

Fast-forward a few months.

My 18-year-old daughter announced she had decided to travel solo around Europe for seven weeks. 'No' should have been the first response to come to my sensible, practical parenting mind. But here's the thing: I had no problem with the decision she had made. I trusted her implicitly as I had observed the way she had been planning this trip, meticulously researching every step, from hostels to the places she would be visiting. On top of all this, she had been reading every blog available written by other solo travellers who had undertaken the same journey. I had no doubt that she was well-informed and competent enough to take on such an adventure.

However, a number of well-meaning friends were trying to convince me that this might not be the most sensible decision for my teenage daughter. This began to drown out my own voice, whilst the outside voices were getting louder. The truth was I did not feel a single ounce of anxiety for allowing her to do this. So why did I feel so guilty? Why was self-doubt daring to creep in uninvited, whilst all the time I wanted to shout, 'It's fine, I trust her'?

We spend too much time looking outside of ourselves, and too little time deciphering our inner voice. Too often we listen to others, allowing their views and assessments to influence our own lives and values. To shut out those voices and turn up the volume of our own voice seems inconceivable. And yet, ours is the only voice that matters.

Who is going to know you better than you do?

In trusting my daughter to follow the path she had chosen, I empowered her. Isn't empowerment a far more precious element to hand down to our children than prized family heirlooms? So I shut out the outside voices, released my control over the situation and trusted, because I believed deeply that all would be fine. In fact, in the seven weeks that my daughter was travelling, I *loved* receiving pictures of the places she was visiting and looked forward to the exciting conversations we'd have on the phone about her days spent exploring Europe, experiencing new cultures and connecting with people, making new friendships in a way she could never have done had she travelled with someone else. She was safe and happy, and more importantly, the trip gave her a sense of confidence she had never known before.

I don't mean to sound smug in any way, but I had known all along that this would be the case. My gut instinct had reassured me. But had I listened to the external voices telling me what I should feel and what being a 'responsible' parent looked like, my daughter would have been deprived of this amazing experience.

If we dilute the influence that conversations and relationships with others have over our lives and really dare to go within ourselves, we will emerge with the answer – the *true* answer – that we are looking for. Meditation, yoga and mindfulness can all help us to listen to our gut and quieten our thinking, but the key is to turn the volume up on our inner voice, even if it's just by a notch. A 5% difference can change everything, teasing out more of who we are, what we value and what we would like to express. Then we can become more robust, developing a strong foundation that will make decision making less of a stressful pursuit and more of true knowing.

11: Innate Wellbeing

I learn so much from the people I work with, and I was reminded of this when I became reacquainted with a Somali teenager who had been a therapy client over 10 years ago. I had first met him as a child when he arrived in the UK from war-torn Somalia.

He had initially been separated from his father as they left Somalia and had moved to a number of European locations before reaching London. As you can well imagine, he was feeling deeply anxious, confused and displaced. At the time, I was working for a superb organisation as a Project Manager in charge of therapy services at a large school with a diverse mix of pupils. When this child's file landed on my desk, I remember planning our first session with some trepidation.

On meeting him for the first time, I observed a somewhat underweight nine-year-old child who could barely make eye contact. He was withdrawn, spoke little English, found social interactions difficult, and spent most of his time hiding from people, generally preferring isolation. Although he was difficult to engage with, I welcomed him into our therapy service with open arms. I observed how vulnerable he was and how much he needed attention and support. His parents, although well-meaning, spoke very basic English and were struggling with their own displacement issues, finding British culture to be worlds away from their own.

Throughout my time working with this child and becoming more involved with his family, I often wondered if refugee children from war-torn countries ever recovered from their past and carved out a better future. I had to hold the hope alive for this child, so I removed my professional hat and didn't focus on diagnosing him. I simply treated him with the decency and humanity that he deserved.

I have never forgotten our sessions, but as with any client, there came a time when I had to let him go and trust that he would find his own way in life – until a chance meeting 10 years later reacquainted us. I bumped into him recently with his father in a packed shopping centre. Much to my delight, as soon as the boy, now an extremely tall 19-year-old, saw me, his eyes brightened up in recognition.

I felt a huge wave of emotion as he announced (with his dad watching on proudly) that he was studying English at Cambridge University. My eyes welled up as I observed this young man in front of me who had seemed so vulnerable all those years ago, yet now had reached the pinnacle of the academic world. What an incredible example of what human beings are capable of.

This certainly challenged the myths that I had been familiar with when working in psychology.

YOUR EARLY YEARS DETERMINE HOW YOU WILL TURN OUT. The early stages in life have the potential to affect the rest of your life, but only if you allow them to. Your state of mind and the thinking you have about your past experiences will determine which direction you will head in. If you carry your past like a rucksack full of heavy stones, this is how you will experience life moving forward. The past will drag you back, and the psychological weight will be almost too much to bear.

I have worked with clients who suffered the most unbelievable neglect in the early years of their lives. Some became destructive, vindictive and bitter, but others, who were able to throw off the weight of their past, progressed and became determined never to repeat the errors of their parents.

HUMAN BEINGS ARE BROKEN AND NEED FIXING FROM THEIR PSYCHOLOGICAL AILMENTS. When I reflect on the Somali child, I could easily have viewed him as broken and needing psychological help. Instead, I saw him as essentially healthy, both mentally and physically; he was simply unsettled and needed time to adjust to his new environment. He needed empathy, patience and understanding, not a diagnosis he would be stuck with for the rest of his life.

I hold back on emotional diagnoses at most levels, because the reality is that once someone is diagnosed, they're stuck with a label which is pretty hard to shake off.

No matter how broken, confused, displaced or anxious someone might appear, there is always hope. There is no way I could have imagined the anxious, underweight child from Somalia would progress to Cambridge University, but he proved himself right and the world wrong. He blossomed beyond his past and carved out a successful future for himself.

We don't define people by the state they are currently in. They are much more than this. We need to be able to connect with a person's potential. Where they see themselves as an insignificant acorn, we need to see an oak tree. People pick up how we relate to them, and we can't pretend to empathise or care; it's conveyed through our actions and body language. This is what made it so magical for me to bump into a former client who survived their emotional condition and is now a thriving Cambridge University student.

12: Leadership Through Self-Mastery

A while back, I attended a workshop on leadership, love and power with a number of other coaches. The experience awakened a question within me: What type of impact do I want to make through leadership?

Before stepping into leadership and influencing others, we first have to shine a light on ourselves. The quest for leadership becomes an inner journey to discover who we are and what we care about, and this demands a high degree of self-mastery. If we don't know what our own values and expectations are, how can we possibly set goals for others and lead by example? Until we look inside ourselves, it's not possible to look at others and recognise their potential.

Essentially, we're all leaders in some shape or form. From the moment we rise in the morning, we are leading by creating the energy that fills our day. Our energy is dictated by what we choose to focus on, from the most mundane things to the most profound. We are leading the most important creation there is: our lives. Interacting with the environment as a hapless victim will not serve us well as we step into creative leadership.

Everything changes when we're not waiting for someone else

to lead. This covers body language and the words we use to describe our reality. It is also influenced by our focus and general approach to life, practically as well as psychologically.

Let's think of great leaders such as Mother Teresa, Nelson Mandela and Maya Angelou. None of them had privileged upbringings nor positions of power initially; what made them great leaders was that they were clear about their missions. They were authentic to their causes, took courageous stands, and had strong values and beliefs which overrode everything else.

For leadership to work, you need to be fully familiar with your weaknesses and strengths. What has influenced you so much that you can potentially go on to inspire and influence others? Do you have the courage of your convictions? Are you able to stand up for your beliefs? For others to climb on to your platform, they must feel that it is robust and not going to collapse at any second. You need to be authentic, as nobody will be convinced unless you convey a sense of genuine commitment to a deep cause. Until you know what you want to do and why you want to do it, your leadership will be superficial.

Believing you matter will allow you to treat everyone else as if they matter too. This is a winning combination for any leader, whether you're managing your life and interacting with the day to day, or leading a team. As evidence suggests, true leaders don't need a system of hierarchy. The key is to surround yourself with great role models who lead in the way you would like to, as this will allow you to strive for better.

If you feel inspired by individuals who are influential within their fields, contact them. Enquire and you will learn from them. Whatever knowledge you gain, you can integrate into your own style of leadership, making it personal to you. I have done this a number of times, and it's surprising how receptive successful people are to anyone making contact with them for a few words of wisdom.

The art of great leadership is not to change who you are, but express the best of who you are to inspire others to do so too. Tap into your own limitless potential and draw this out in others too. It is easier to lead when people feel great around you.

13: Face Fear Head on

Have you ever prevented yourself from pursuing something – be it travelling, applying for a job, a new course, or venturing into the unknown – due to fear? If you have, you're in good company. Many people feel fear or discomfort when they're taking on something new or leaving their comfort zone. This fear, often coming from an irrational place, binds them to their safety routine and prevents them from evolving and developing any further.

Fear can feel paralysing at times. There is something about navigating into the unknown that has a powerful hold on us, and no matter how hard our urge to move on may be, this hold tends to win hands down.

Most of us are driven by an insatiable yearning for new knowledge and experiences – to go where we have never ventured before, both physically and emotionally. I was reminded of this recently when I was stopped by police officers at an airport in Detroit on my way to Nashville. In my rushed attempt to get everything ready for my trip to the US, I had assumed my visa application had been accepted (note to self – never assume). The visa application process is pretty stringent, so there I was being escorted by a number of burly officers from the customs desk.

They walked me into a room already occupied by unsuspecting travellers of diverse cultures. My fear was twofold: I was scared of what they would do to me, and I was afraid I might miss my connecting flight.

Finding yourself in a foreign country seems to exacerbate the problem – every question the officer asked sounded like an accusation. I realised that when we are afraid of a situation, our minds are clogged up with fearful thoughts and alarmist projections into the future, and this gets in the way of working towards a creative solution.

The moment I understood that I would have to calm down to find a way out of this, I took a few deep breaths and began to speak to the officer. I asked him about his work, I told him how much I was looking forward to going to Nashville – basically I used a degree of schmooze without going over the top.

Within less than an hour, the officer suddenly stood up, walked up to the computer, typed away and graciously completed a new visa application, asked for the fee, printed off the visa and handed it to me with what seemed like the semblance of a smile on his face.

And yes, I managed to catch my next flight by the skin of my teeth.

Essentially, our fear emanates directly from fearful thinking – jumbled information we project into the non-existent future – and this gives us a warped view of events. I was already imagining what jail time in Detroit would look like, when this was far from being what would happen next. When we take fear seriously, we can become emotionally paralysed and closed up, rather than tackling the origins of the problem and finding a creative solution. It's okay to feel fear – we just need to acknowledge it and work past it. A few words of warning, though: this doesn't apply to dangerous stunts or placing yourself in truly terrifying situations. It's about conquering irrational fears, which may take the form of facing up to a customs officer (as in my case), facing spiders or public speaking.

Don't wait until fear goes away. Face it – head on. Navigate into the unknown beyond the boundaries. This is the only way you will realise that your fearful thoughts are worse than reality. Way worse.

Reflect on any times you have attempted the unthinkable and realised all your fears were exaggerated. You more than likely completed the task with a sense of relief and elation. In these moments, you went beyond your fears and showed them up for what they really are.

My experiences of working through fear have often been successful, and each time I'm rewarded by a bubbling sense of total and utter achievement. It's an adrenalin rush like nothing else. Experiences I would never have dared to attempt before, and felt I was incapable of achieving, all became positive and emotionally uplifting once I'd pushed past the initial boundaries of my own fearful thoughts.

14: Self-Doubt Must Be Crushed

In 1975, Freddie Mercury wrote 'Bohemian Rhapsody' at his home in London. He wrote the first part and went out to eat his dinner. The rest of the song was written on his return. Fellow musicians told him that it would never be a hit and no radio station would dare play it. It was deemed too long – at just under six minutes. The verses were fatalistic and included an odd set up, comprising of an intro, a ballad segment, an operatic passage, a hard rock break and a reflective coda.

The song catapulted Queen from being rock stars into mega gods, and it became one of the best-selling singles of all time.

From what I understand, Freddie Mercury dug in his heels when presenting his masterpiece, and refused to succumb to the opinions of others. The piece was an anomaly, but he trusted himself, his art and the direction he was moving into musically. You could say he had a high degree of certainty and self-confidence. In response, the listening public was hooked from start to finish. Many have speculated about what the song means, but since it has given us decades of pleasure, frankly I don't care and wouldn't bother to pick it apart. It simply *is*.

This is a great lesson in determination and crushing self-doubt.

How many times have we been told not to follow a particular path or a situation that feels bizarre and unhinged at the time? But when we are overcome by a sense of certainty, there is no room for self-doubt to come sneaking in through the back door. At times we need to behave like a boxer, punching until his opponent is comatose. We must beat self-doubt senseless so that it cannot arise and badger us again with its never-ending mindless chatter.

I'm sure we have all had times in our lives when self-doubt has crept in like an unwanted guest after closing time. It lurks around, creating a vibe which has the potential to drag us down into the gutter – a pretty familiar place to be. It shadows us, following us around with its blabbering discouragement, a constant reminder that if our idea is rejected, we must retreat bashfully back to home base. It pulls us towards pleasing others and away from where we feel naturally pulled. Self-doubt is the catalyst for an intense amount of frustration that permeates the very air we breathe.

Ask yourself, what is your 'Bohemian Rhapsody'? What is encased in an idea, piece of art, or creation you would love to share?

Imagine how much richer the world would be with the one thing you can offer that no one else can. If you could assert your certainty that what you want is right, what could be possible for you? Self-doubt pulls you back from truly impacting others. If you allow the idea, the gift, the art form to flow through you without the contamination of doubtful thought, can you imagine the result?

We need to let go of self-doubt and hang on to our own personal moment of certainty as if our lives depended on it. Because it does. Without it, our stroke of genius fizzles out and dies a slow, painful death.

Certainty needs to breathe from a place of true knowing that however many doors get slammed and however many negative responses we receive, we will continue to knock on other more welcoming doors. We must persevere and believe in what we want, developing a sense of certainty even if anxiety and mayhem descend.

I know that I would have been all the poorer if 'Bohemian Rhapsody' hadn't been blaring out of my cassette recorder in the eighties. In the midst of my turbulent teenage years, it represented diversity, difference, exploration and pushing boundaries in a powerful way. It represented one man's definition of true art, not in the conventional sense, but in the manner that Freddie Mercury decided it should be. What a great role model for adolescents.

The action required of you is to begin to quieten the self-doubt and give your potential greatness a louder voice.

15: Choose Yourself

I once heard that in the early part of the 12th century, the famous St Mark's Square in Venice was adorned with countless spoils taken from ancient Turkey, Rome, and further afield. The Venetians laid claim to these treasures as rightfully theirs, proudly displaying them in ownership. If this is true, then it must have taken a certain measure of *chutzpah* – which translates into determination, pro-activity and tenacity.

We can learn so much from this. What if we were to stake a claim on our talents and capabilities, and display them in the same way the Venetians displayed the treasures? Instead, many people hide their talents in a casket for all eternity whilst watching enviously as others rise up and claim the glory. Could we possibly claim the title of best sales representative, marketing specialist, or leading coach in an industry? Could we possibly be so bold as to choose ourselves?

This isn't a 'fake it until you make it' process. The key is to claim our expertise, and then begin truly owning it, committing ourselves to excelling in that area and embodying what we represent. But often what occurs is we wait to *be chosen*. We wait for someone of importance to hand us the coveted title, further inciting an intense need for external validation. It simply isn't enough to value ourselves and claim our talents.

But why not claim them for ourselves?

I recently met a speaker at a networking event who claimed to be the best speaker in Europe. I had never met him previously or even heard him give a presentation, so I could not comment on his talent. Even he didn't know with certainty that he was the best, but he still proudly claimed the title like a boxer claiming the heavyweight belt and raising it up for all to see.

Choosing yourself might have selfish connotations. However, it doesn't need to be so. Think of it this way: it's simply a way of standing up for something you know you can offer, then choosing a course of action and striving to develop it further.

One of the biggest impediments to choosing ourselves is a fear of rejection. Instead we become acceptable, pleasing to others, and, frankly, forgettable. We mask who we are in an attempt to win contracts, clients, relationships and love. This isn't claiming what we can really offer, though; this is simply wearing a costume, like the Venetians during the Charlevoix Venetian Festival, which is filled with colour and pageantry, but little else.

I spent the first few years of my career attending endless meetings, events and talks in the hope that someone would make a surprise discovery. But at times, one of the most powerful and self-affirming actions we can take is to stop waiting. Instead, we need to go ahead, develop value for what we create and carve out a place at the table – or even create our own table and decide whom we want to have sitting next to us. This is far more empowering and pro-active than the waiting game.

We are no longer in primary school where we wait for teachers to hand out accolades for the best behaved student, star sports player or star student of the week. We might still live by the same rules and therefore wait for the acknowledgement and validation before we take action and stake a claim for what we stand for.

Staking a claim is not in any way shallow or lacking in integrity, but it does need to be accompanied by a commitment to learning, development and growth. As the Venetians built a beautiful, unique and mesmerising city, despite supposedly having staked a claim on the treasures of others, we too must do everything in our power to build around the claim we make as a way of creating a solid and robust foundation.

16: Giving Up Is Not an Option

Bruce Lee arrived in the United States of America in 1959 as a nameless immigrant with $115 in his pocket. Within 20 years, *Time Magazine* had named him one of the 100 most influential people of the 20th century, and 8 June was proclaimed Bruce Lee Day in Los Angeles. This seems nothing short of a miracle when we reflect on Bruce's journey, which was full of misfortunes and challenges. Nevertheless, Bruce embodied a life of purpose, and his example provides a great inspiration for others to embrace their limitless potential. His was not a fast-paced success story, but one in which he slowly perfected his craft to become known worldwide as a martial artist with a warrior spirit.

When he was asked to describe his unique style, he answered, 'My style? You can call it the art of fighting without fighting.'

In a fight, he calmly stood firm and responded to his opponent's moves. Bruce was a dynamic master. This became the way he anchored himself when times were hard.

So what can we learn from Bruce Lee?

He didn't give up, despite becoming paralysed at the height of his fame. It didn't deter him when he was plagued with intense physical pain, which he overcame by leaving notes all around the house saying, 'Go on!' He found an anchor which kept him rooted to what he wanted to achieve.

Imagine a boat gently floating on the waves, but it can't drift off too far into the ocean as its anchor brings it straight back to shore. Your anchor is the part of you which is untouched by failure, regrets and recriminations. It brings you back to what you truly want by increasing your focus and determination.

What is your anchor? What is the one factor keeping you grounded and stopping you from giving up when times get hard?

If you're considering giving up on what you want, connect to what keeps you in the game. You may have entered desperate times, feel humiliated, your balance may be running low and resources waning. The movie playing in the back of your mind could be worthy of an Oscar nomination, such is the acting ability of the imagination.

If there was a martial art to fight the mind's bad habits, I imagine people would be queuing up to learn it. Yet inside every one of us, there is strength, wellbeing and resilience. Our families, businesses and humanity depend on our resilience. A note of caution, though: there are some battles and situations you need to let go of, but there are others that you fully want to step into.

As I look back, it's evident to me that life without meaning, growth or challenges is a life not worth living. Challenges force us to dip into our inner resources and ask deeper questions which can be spiritually enriching. I wouldn't trade what I have now, despite the difficult path I have had to walk, for a stable, staid and numb existence with everything neatly planned, controlled and scheduled. This can feel like a spiritual death. Instead, we need to embrace the sense of energy and alertness and vitality that wakes us up each morning when we've had to walk on fire to get to this point.

It's often too hard to live in uncertainty; to slay the demons that envelop us each time we feel rejected, a venture collapses, a sale falls through, a client drops out, or no one is interested when we launch our shiny new product. We may be looking for more meaning, purpose and happiness in life, but fear and anxiety is a clear invitation to give up too soon. The mind overtakes us like a dense fog and it's impossible to see any further forward. We need to wait until the fog clears and we can then make the next decision with clarity.

Bruce Lee experienced moments of true despair, left with a mere $50 in his pocket when work dried up, forcing him to sell his home. I can imagine him bent over with pain when his body became paralysed, eating a piece of stale bread and a tin of soup for sustenance at his lowest point. But perseverance won the battle raging in his mind. Anything else would have kicked him to the ground in a more aggressive way than any of his fighting opponents could have done.

If we give up in our minds, we give up in our bodies, and then the battle is lost. Life happens and it's impossible to stop events unravelling, but we can choose our response. We can connect to the anchor that keeps us firmly in the game and reminds us why we must stay in the game and not give up.

17: Drop Resistance

One of the sports I've most enjoyed learning in the past year was paddle surfing, drifting through the crystal-clear waters of the Mediterranean, following the path of least resistance in the natural flow of the sea. Practising this sport alongside an experienced instructor was probably the most 'in flow' I've ever felt. Our surfboards were in sync, one never obstructing the other, each of us following the spontaneous action of the waves and responding accordingly.

This underlined a way of being that doesn't come naturally to me: a mixture of trust, surrender and open receiving. I had no idea how tough this passiveness would be, and I noticed that up to that point, I'd held a deep level of resistance which had unconsciously seeped into most areas of my life.

How I paddle surfed that day is how I, moving forwards, aim to navigate my way through life.

Kellie Kuecha, master of business branding and identity, stated, 'How we do one thing is how we do everything.' Our character or nature dictates how we handle all the day-to-day things in life, no matter how small.

As I listened attentively to the paddle surfing instructor, initially I wanted to ignore his instructions and do my own thing, overtaking him and impressing as a smarty pants. Instead, I decided to follow his lead – or rather, mirror him whilst using my individuality and intuition to stay firmly on the board. I feared a wave would throw me off my surfboard, but I stayed on not by fighting it, but by finding the most stable part of the board – the centre. Did I fall into the sea? Countless times. But each time I climbed back on to the surfboard, my resolve had strengthened and my technique was sounder. It surprised me how much I loved the beauty of being in full flow with the water, which carried me wherever I needed to go, trusting the natural order and being guided by the peaks of each wave, surrendering to what might emerge and responding accordingly.

The experience reminded me of how we often try to navigate a thousand paces beyond where we should be, all the time missing what is happening in between.

Imagine if we could fall into situations, pick ourselves up and aim to do it better next time, confidently navigating the spontaneous waves of life. There is a beauty and wisdom in being guided by the path of least resistance, following the natural energy to see where it takes us, allowing ourselves to let go of control. There is a dance between doing and being, each taking its turn to lead, and sometimes we have to let life be the leading dance partner. An experience is made a lot harder by continuous resistance, attempting to go against the order of the flow. But isn't that what we often do?

Following the path of least resistance is something I see people stumble on, and it's something I have struggled with myself. There is a misconception that the only way to live is to work hard, but what if life was easier than this? Granted, life can throw horrendous things in our path – it's thrown a few nasty situations at me over the past few years. But during the times I've surrendered more, trusted and simply let go, difficult though it has been, what has emerged has been far more fruitful and authentic than if I'd struggled against the flow.

Let go of control, allowing your true nature to emerge effortlessly.

Notice those who pace up and down, complaining and throwing their weight about when a flight is cancelled, a doctor's appointment rescheduled or illness strikes. Observe how much energy they waste battling against the inevitable, and compare it with those who choose to surrender to the natural flow of events.

A few months ago, I was volunteering at a refugee centre in London. I'm constantly struck by how much I learn from those who have lived for so long with uncertainty that it has become a way of being. The refugee's life is a process of never-ending surrender. They are at the mercy of a system which either decides to allow them into the country, or spits them out with no consideration for their humanity.

Whilst at the refugee centre, I was speaking to a Nigerian lady the same age as myself. She had been living in the UK for 10 years in one room which had been kindly offered to her. All that time waiting to receive a letter from the Home Office where she hoped she would be allowed to remain in the country.

She had been a nurse in Nigeria and had been hoping to work in the UK upon her arrival. During her 10-year wait, she had not been allowed to return to her place of birth to visit her family; she could not earn money as she had no way of setting up a bank account and had no family around to support her. I found it truly unthinkable to imagine not seeing my family for 10 years. The level of isolation she must have experienced is beyond my comprehension.

Yet this lady was one of the most divine people I have met. I distinctly remember her tears as she shared how grateful she was to have the refugee centre to visit once a month. There she had been able to meet others dealing with the same issues as herself.

I asked her how she found the strength to carry on without any support systems in place. She responded that she always had the end in mind and focused on this. Not for one moment did she allow herself to feel negativity, otherwise she would have fallen apart. She had to keep it together to see the process through.

During the final week I was with her, she received a letter from the Home Office which sealed her fate. She had been granted a status and permission to work. Now she could finally allow herself to feel the effects of what she had been through over those difficult years.

I meet so many like her who sit in uncertainty for years. Their surrender is absolute. They are so used to not being defined by their possessions or bank balances that their resilience is at a level most of us will never know. I am humbled by those who can feel gratitude, be gracious and find a way to say thank you in the face of uncertainty.

When I contrast this with people who complain that their custom-made kitchen arrived a week late, or a spa hotel they booked was not up to their expectations, I feel a need to walk away from the conversation. .

Maintaining a stable disposition and simply surrendering, even when life throws us the unthinkable, can be hugely challenging at first. As we practise this, even in the tiniest of areas, it slowly begins to absorb itself into larger areas of our reality.

Life isn't defined by what we can control. It is defined by all the times when we get thrown off the board and graciously readjust ourselves, resolving to learn lessons. Trust that the path of least resistance is the most effective way to a life of joy and self-expression.

Part Three
CHANGE DIRECTION

18: Lose Your Way Without Losing Your Mind

There is an epidemic sweeping the nation. It's not an illness; it's not a contagious disease. It's actually a phrase I often hear other people utter and, to my chagrin, have uttered myself over the years. The phrase goes like this:

'I don't know what to do.'

This epidemic plagued our teenage years; however to my surprise, I am hearing it more and more often from the middle-aged sector.

There is a feeling of having been cheated.

When we were in high school, we were asked to choose our exam subjects, and assured that passing these exams would lead to university. A degree would ensure (we were told) a job, security and a life all nicely mapped out in front of us. All we had to do, after being armed with all these qualifications, was to go out there and grab what we wanted.

How wrong we were.

More middle-aged people than ever are requiring coaching sessions to mull over the question that occupies their every waking moment: 'What do I do next?'

Essentially, there comes a time in life when a pretty uncomfortable feeling called dissatisfaction brews underneath what, on the surface, looks like a great life. If you have talents in many different areas, this can be even more confusing. Why would you choose to utilise one talent and not another?

When clients come for coaching sessions and elaborate on their difficulties with making a decision or knowing where to head next, detailing everything they have done in the past few years, I ask them to stop mid-flow. This normally takes them by surprise, but they are listing technicalities and problems arising from their intellect. I ask them to be silent for a few minutes to access something deeper and more meaningful.

Then I ask them a simple question: 'What do you really want?'

The answer that comes from their heart is generally slow and measured, since we have moved out of their intellectual realm and into a place of calm self-reflection. I am constantly taken aback by the wisdom that pours out of my clients during these sessions. Instead of a barrage of content which has no substance, they generally come up with something pretty simplistic, such as more freedom, more family time, or even more fun.

For many people, fun and excitement are buried under a sea of responsibilities. I notice a change as they speak; their eyes brighten and a different energy takes over. The dull look on their faces transforms into an aliveness that hasn't seen the light of day for many a year.

The question is, 'What do you do when you don't know what to do?'

The answer may disappoint you and leave you feeling somewhat deflated if what you want are solutions, a rule book and an answer that is as clear as daylight. But sometimes enlightenment requires space, time and patience, and it may well come to you in the most unsuitable of places.

I remember losing my bearings a while back, so I decided to speak to my mentor, who was an expert in the subject of clarity. I explained how unmotivated I felt and that I didn't know what the next step in my professional life should be. His response was soothing, measured and full of simple wisdom when he said:

'The only problem you have is seeing your lack of motivation and losing your bearings as a problem.'

This was simple, yet profound. He encouraged me to do what felt right. If my body required a hiatus right then I should listen to it rather than resist it.

I was reluctant initially as my answer for not knowing what to do had always been to do more, be more and achieve more. This of course provided a momentary distraction as I became involved in new ventures, but they meant nothing and went nowhere since the only motivation I had was to do for the sake of doing. During these times, I would usually buy more books (Amazon made a killing in sales), enrol on more courses and take on work that I was completely disinterested in. But doing anything felt better than doing nothing.

Then I decided to do something different. I stopped.

My gut feeling was suggesting I travel to Marrakesh in Morocco for a few days. This seemed ludicrous, as Morocco is not really the ideal place for a woman to walk around alone. But I ignored that sensible piece of advice as I trusted my gut more than I trusted the travel guide books. As a child growing up in Gibraltar, I had spent most summers going to Morocco on holiday with my family. I remember feeling at my most alive and happy in this place. I loved the rich, exotic smells and the culture, as well as the warm hospitality we always received.

I was an intensely curious child, and since this curiosity knew no bounds, when I was six years old my parents lost my brother and me in the midst of Morocco. Fortunately, they found us a few hours later in the desert with a Moroccan Berber whom I had befriended, where I was safely perched on his camel having the time of my life. Danger, anxiety and fear of the unknown didn't exist for me in those days; they developed over time as the beauty of curiosity and passion was crushed by predictability, stability, structure and the known.

After speaking to my mentor, I listened to my gut, ignored my well-meaning friends and family and set off on my own. As I arrived in Morocco, the curious and fearless six-year-old child I had left behind returned. I nourished it by hiring a tour guide who took me through every nook and cranny of the area. And my lost wisdom came back to me. Not in the office at home, or in a meeting, but in the isolation of the Moroccan Atlas Mountains.

I was venturing through the isolated mountain track, and as I stood there in the company of a couple of goats, a thought came to me so strongly that it took my breath away. It came out in a gentle voice: 'You need to start sharing your writing.'

This seemed ridiculous at the time. Although I had written copious amounts in diaries and journals over the years, I hadn't written anything else for a while because personal issues (I told myself) had blocked my writing flow. I had never had the confidence to share what I wrote anyway as it was too exposing. But this urge came to me so strongly that as soon as I returned to London, I took action by publishing a few articles online, which led to a number of personal development websites contacting me to ask me to write for them.

I soon noticed that there was a different energy to my work. It was not born out of anxiety, but out of deep connection. In a short space of time, I became a guest contributor to a number of online publications, wrote a chapter for a business book, engaged more coaching clients through my writing and that year was shortlisted for a national writing award.

Not bad for someone who didn't know what to do.

There have been times since when I have not known what to do, so I take a step back and don't rush into making decisions.

My life has taken on a more reflective flavour, and my decisions are no longer made from anxiety or a place of urgency. Things can wait and I can linger in the unknown for far longer than I ever have before.

There is a benefit in the known – it feels safe, but that's only because it's known, certainly not because it's better. Losing your bearings has its benefits, even though it can feel scary and exposing at times. The reality is that there is no compass in life; we have no rule book. Ultimately, you decide which direction you follow. It's that simple. When you understand this, you will realise that, in essence, you are never really lost. You are, in fact, precisely where you need to be.

Listen to yourself (your gut feeling). Try it. I can't promise it will be comfortable, but boy, will you grow.

19: Navigating a Personal Tsunami

I was fortunate enough to be in Thailand for the tenth anniversary of the tsunami that left a trail of devastation throughout most of south east Asia. I experienced a beautiful ceremony of remembrance on Patong Beach in Phuket where survivors returned to heal from the trauma of the past and release lanterns into the sky as a way of remembering those who did not return.

Gazing out at boats swaying in the light breeze on the ocean, a stunning backdrop of mountains and palm trees behind me, I found it impossible to imagine the destruction that had unfolded on that Boxing Day. The perpetrator was water – a usually calm and graceful element that can so easily slip through our fingers, yet as a collective force it loses its grace, calm, and beauty. That fateful day, water fiercely destroyed everything in its path with no mercy whatsoever, no questions asked, because nature works in this way. It does what it needs to do, at times without any warning. We are always at its mercy.

An important lesson that arose from this natural disaster was the power of the traumatised, helpless and vulnerable inhabitants to pick up the few pieces they had left and rebuild from the rubble; to start anew when they had lost everything except their lives. Having recently emerged from a divorce and being in the process of rebuilding after the emotional destruction, I began to reflect on life.

If we were to lose everything that we believe defines us, would this mean we'd lose our ability to feel valued in society?

This question led to a deeper level of soul searching. I realised that at times there is value in loss, however painful and difficult it may be, because we usually lose what didn't serve us well in the first place. In essence, if we can live without what we think defines us, then we can experience the world in a totally different way, creating an incredible sense of freedom.

It is interesting to examine the way we view our worth in the western world. If we do not meet the criteria we set for ourselves – the top-of-the-range car, the plush home, the high-flying career – what then? What happens when personal tsunamis hit which have the potential to destroy a perfect-looking reality? What will our standpoint be then? Will we analyse why it happened? Or pick apart our childhoods to find someone to blame? Where do we go from here?

There is actually nowhere to go. Not to the past and not to the future. We just have to stay with it as our personal tsunami unfolds. In order to recover, heal and rebuild, we have to suspend the questions. At times, there is simply no answer. And this is the hardest thing to accept when we're trying to rationalise an event as a thinking, feeling human being. We usually feel we need a reason, a motive that satisfies the intellect before we can move on and heal.

It might be important to write your questions without seeking answers. In my experience, the questions answer themselves organically as time progresses. Not everything needs to have the urgency we expect. As children, we were asked questions in the classroom by our teachers and had to give an immediate answer. For you now, there is a real value in just articulating these questions and seeing what happens.

We have the capacity to heal from a life tsunami. Life does not pick on us personally, like a force of nature, it just happens. If we spend time pulling the personal difficulties that life inflicts on us apart, we will only block the healing process. It's like picking away at a scab.

I learnt a great deal from the survivors I encountered in Thailand as they spoke about the way the devastation had hit the country at its heart. There was an incredible amount of grief initially, which was important and appropriate. But rather than asking why their loved ones had been swept away and their homes destroyed, they focused on preventing a similar disaster happening in the future; on making sure they had a more robust evacuation system and better emergency structures in place.

Is that not what we all need to do when life strikes a blow? Ensure we learn from the situation and build a more solid inner foundation to prevent it from happening again, rather than take it as a personal attack on our worth.

20: Astonishment Trumps Expectation

If I had to reflect on one issue underpinning many of the frustrations which plague people, it would be their unreasonable levels of expectation. So many people expect life to be different and can't comprehend why they constantly feel deflated and downtrodden.

Whilst reflecting on this problem, I realised that expectation revolves around a belief that is centred in the future which may or may not be realistic; this then gives rise to the emotion of disappointment. When checking out the opposite meaning of 'expectation' online, I was surprised to see the word 'astonishment' flash up on my computer screen.

After my initial surprise, I realised that it made complete sense. The moment we suspend our expectations and step away from what 'should be', we can become fully present in the world around us. This leaves the door wide open to experience gratitude, astonishment and wonder at what we have right here in this moment. We stop looking for how the world can give us our 'entitlement package'.

Expectations don't allow us to be fully present in the moment. Instead, we're either focused on the past and what should have been, or running after a non-existent future. By dropping expectations, we shift our internal world in a different direction, and this can have monumental results.

There is a common narrative of expectations: 'My boss should be different', 'I should be married by now', 'My children should behave', 'My team should respect me'. Whenever we use the word 'should', it's normally a sign that we're sitting on an expectation. These weigh us down like a lead balloon – a balloon everyone else is left holding. Expectations create an illusion of control as we set rules for how life, people, society and work need to be, and everyone else has to live up to them, even if they don't know what we're expecting. This can lead to anger, disappointment and resentment.

We all have the choice to communicate and agree these with other people. We can then renegotiate if need be. The great thing about this is that everything is out in the open, and everyone knows in advance what to expect.

Reflect on your life. If something you expected hasn't come to fruition, you now have two choices. You can go round in circles, focusing on the life you feel you should be entitled to, or you can start using the tools you have, to create the life you want.

Ask yourself, 'If what I expected isn't in my life, how have I kept it away? What choices did I make along the way that evolved into my current reality? How do I need to show up in each area of my life to take me one step nearer to what I desire?' This moves you away from consistently digging the 'expectation hole' as there's nothing you will find there, and into the realm of taking responsibility.

Moving swiftly on to astonishment. When I coach clients to let go of expectation, what I really do is coach them to be astonished throughout their lives, no matter what transpires externally. This transforms their world and everything they create.

The moment you start looking ahead, and enjoy the present moment, life looks completely different. I recommend you shift your focus, as life will then have a different colour, flavour and feel to it.

PRACTISE GRATITUDE. Make this a daily practice. Show gratitude for all the aspects of your life you take for granted. It will transform how you view your current circumstances.

The Miracle Morning by Hal Elrod is one of the best books I've found that recommends practising a sense of wonder and astonishment before 8am. If you commit to transforming your early mornings, I can promise you that it will impact how you show up for the rest of the day. *The Power of Now* by Eckhart Tolle is also a great book about being present and showing gratitude.

VOLUNTARY WORK. This cultivates a feeling of giving back to the community, as well as giving you the opportunity to speak to people who have overcome huge hurdles with limited resources.

I recently encouraged a coaching client to volunteer for the elderly. He had previously expected other people to love him and was constantly feeling empty and disappointed inside. I arranged a placement for him to show him that he needed to give love in order to receive it.

He came back transformed. He realised he had so much love to give and what joy there is in giving it, and he had enjoyed loving the elderly and listening to their inspiring stories.

MEDITATE. Spend quality time in silence. Even just five minutes early in the morning can make a world of difference. Meditating, going inward, breathing deeply and connecting to your core will bring acceptance and stop you surrendering to what you expect.

Resist the temptation to be constantly on your phone, reacting to every message. Instead, take a walk in silence and observe the world around you. You're likely to be amazed at how attuned you will be to every tiny noise, from the birds singing and leaves rustling, to the traffic driving by. This brings presence, gratitude, astonishment and wonder to your day.

If you're expecting love, start by giving more love. If you're expecting others to treat you as if you're worthy, behave as if you are. When you change your expectations of the world and its responsibility for your wellbeing, you lower your sense of entitlement. This releases you to enjoy freedom, astonishment, fulfilment and joy.

21: Make Momentum Your New Mindset

I was sitting on a long haul flight from London to Chicago. Despite having a fear of flying, I began to reflect on momentum whilst sitting in some pretty heavy turbulence. I visualised an aircraft accumulating enough power to take off from the ground.

As the aircraft begins to move, it slowly gathers engine power and speed. As these increase, the accumulation of power allows for one of the greatest man-made miracles to launch itself into the sky. But imagine if the aircraft gathered speed and then stopped, or even worse, reduced speed to such an extent that there was not enough power to lift it into the sky.

The aircraft analogy holds well when we're considering our dreams, desires and ideas. Although they might seem great at the time, there is often a drop in momentum between the initial idea and the execution. I don't necessarily mean we should rush into ventures blindly, firing on all cylinders; I'm speaking about momentum gathered over time from the conscious deployment of actions. This momentum is built on habits and behaviours that take us from where we are now to where we want to be in the future.

In order to create momentum, we need an intention and a purpose that is bigger than ourselves. We need a feeling of devotion and desire to create a greater path and step out of our default reality, and we need to want it really badly.

Think about your desires. How much do you want them? How much do you want to launch your ideas? An aircraft doesn't have a thinking mechanism to halt it in its tracks, but you do.

Often when I'm in conversation with people, they speak about all the things they desire and what their vision is for success. But they go silent when I ask them, 'What are you willing to do to create what you want?'

If you want to create something different, it is essential that you do something different. Doing what you've been doing all your life is only going to give you the same result, and this is where many people get stuck. They're often not willing to do things differently, to push past fears or insecurities to get what they want.

Transporting yourself into a different domain and pushing past your comfort zone will bring with it fear and anxiety. You may believe that this is a clear signal that you have taken a step too far. This is not the case. It's simply your body waking you up to the fact that you've reached a point in your existence which feels strange, uncomfortable and unknown. Like wearing a different type of outfit or fancy dress, it's unsettling and feels unlike you, and the only way the body knows to interpret this is to send a red warning light to stop.

I call it 'thinking paralysis'. An overwhelming accumulation of thinking covers up the essence of who you are, and more importantly, who you could be. Unless you're in a seriously dangerous situation, there is no reason not to proceed, but this accumulation of thinking effectively paralyses you.

The way to negotiate this is to slow down and ask yourself, 'How have these thoughts served me so far?' They actually keep you entrenched in your story so far, but are never useful when you're creating a new one.

There is a moment in life when you have to take stock and commit to either being in the game or stepping out gracefully. Being in the game is going to bring about thinking paralysis moments. Don't cower in the corner; come into the limelight, step by step. This is how momentum builds – by taking deliberate (and at times fearful) action in the same direction for a period of time. This might include making some tough and daunting decisions, but in order to gather momentum, you need to push your mindset into areas you have never gone to previously.

Life is often about pushing past what's uncomfortable, yet in your gut it feels like the right thing to do. You have a deep sense of knowing, albeit not devoid of fear, but the fear is just alerting you to the fact you're in unknown territory, that's all. Don't shy away from it; just thank it for letting you know and carry on. At times you might need extra support to build knowledge in a particular area; this is part of the momentum. It doesn't mean you need to stop.

As I sat on the plane whilst the turbulence subsided, I reminded myself that my fear of flying on an aeroplane colours my thinking and results in the way I perceive my experience. Yet I'm willing to become deeply uncomfortable in order to travel and seek new professional opportunities, as this is part of my momentum. And I will continue to do that which scares me.

It's at the edge of reason that we create something different, and this brings about a sense of aliveness and vibrancy which can't be felt when we're immersed in a controlled existence. Whilst gathering momentum in the midst of freeing ourselves from old thinking, we discover new things about ourselves that we didn't even know existed.

Today, ask yourself which thoughts are preventing you from creating consistent momentum.

22: Overcome Busyness

If you're at the mercy of the busyness epidemic that has spread to global proportions, read on.

Busyness manifests itself in a need to be available to everyone, but the trade-off is an inability to be fully present to anyone at any time. Just ask someone how they are today, and the first answer you'll often get is 'Busy'. It's almost become a medal of achievement; a graduation from the university of life.

More importantly, many people have an aversion to saying, 'I've got some blank spaces in my diary.'

None of the 'busy' people I come into contact with work in hospitals saving lives. They're not firefighters or ambulance staff needed in emergency situations; they're normal people, like you and me. Yet being part of the busyness culture makes them feel important, valued, acknowledged, needed. They feed off this addiction.

For many people, looking at an empty diary is like staring death in the face. Indulging, listening and truly caring become secondary to the external rush of busyness which they have been sucked into. This is the biggest block to relationships between themselves and others.

People get immensely lost in busyness; you can see it in their every move, their every sentence, their body language and way of operating in the world. There is a general air of tension when you're around them. It's as if they would rather be elsewhere as their phone pings or rings every few minutes. They're under the illusion that if only they could be busier, pack their diary even more and be at everyone's beck and call, they would be more confident and self-assured. I still haven't found one single person who has been truly cured of self-esteem issues through busyness. In fact, it seems to exacerbate the problem.

There is a difference between being busy with no purpose and momentum from focused action, and this distinction is crucially important. If what you're doing feels productive and there is a gentle flow, then there is no need to stop. But often the merry-go-round is driven by something that is not innate, and this action is actually pretty destructive. It has no destination or direction, but stays firmly in no man's land, continuing to swivel around aimlessly. It's like putting a cheap plaster on to a gaping wound. The wound will continue to bleed, the plaster providing no benefit whatsoever.

I admit, I have grown up in the Mediterranean, where being laid back and indulging in every moment are our birthright. When I moved to London, I was shocked by the fast pace of people's lives. Even the children had their own schedule of events planned with military precision – guitar practice, gymnastics, dance, homework clubs, and so on. I totally refused from the outset to be dragged into this culture of vacuum-packed arrangements.

As I observed this manic behaviour I saw a troubling phenomenon underlying it, and it smelt of anxiety and fear. I noticed a theme: people were either entrenched in the past or running towards a non-existent future, all the time avoiding what's most important – the present. And an even bigger avoidance – emptiness.

If you identify with this, I understand that asking you to slow down is like asking a bull to stop charging. You likely have no idea how to do this, as you have operated from a place of busyness for a very long time. But ask yourself, are you running towards something or running away from something?

I often find it's the latter.

What's stopping you from creating spaces in your day? What are you resisting? Imagine what it would be like to feel more present in your personal relationships, your business, your friendships, and your world. You would likely feel more vibrant and alive, increasing the quality of your conversations and your level of focus.

Become more alert to your surroundings, which may sound simple, but is hugely effective. Put your phone on silent or switch it off for at least one hour a day. Disable your e-mails for the same period of time. Create boundaries so at times you can be (dare I say it?) unavailable. Start walking more slowly and focus on your surroundings. Make sure you incorporate more of what brings joy into your day (e.g. people, situations and activities). Practise letting go of pleasing everyone.

This isn't about going from super busy to Zen; it's about using different habits to create more space, more flow and more of what you want in your life. Imagine indulging in the moment and tasting a meal with every sense you have (not whilst doing three other things simultaneously); being more present when your child speaks to you; looking at your surroundings and being blown away by their beauty (autumn is doing that for me at the moment); loving and giving your attention fully when you're in the presence of someone else. This means that those around you will receive a full version of you, rather than a diluted version.

23: Self-Imposed Humiliation

People often have feelings of shame or humiliation regarding their past. This could be due to bankruptcy, a business failure, or an unfortunate life situation. These issues prevent people from moving forward and making positive decisions that could change their lives – right now and in the future.

The word shame is derived from 'to cover', and as such, covering oneself – literally or figuratively – is a natural expression of shame. The scientist Charles Darwin in his book *The Expression of the Emotions in Man and Animals* describes the manifestations of shame as blushing, a clouded mind and downcast eyes. They also present themselves in a slack, uneasy posture and a lowered head.

Shame is self-imposed, and so is the guilt that results from believing that we need to get things right all the time. This leads to judging and comparing our actions with unrealistically high standards we've set ourselves, rather than simply experiencing the action with the neutrality it deserves. Every person adds their individual interpretations and approaches.

A number of individuals can go through a similar experience. One will feel exposed, embarrassed and humiliated, whilst others will move swiftly on and remain undisturbed by the whole drama. In the same way we add ingredients and spices to a dish, we each add our own elements to our experiences. As shame and humiliation are subject dependent – shaped by the way we've interpreted and acted upon them – no two people experience these life changers in the same way. Therefore, it is not the experience that is shameful, but the individual person adding their own interpretation to it.

Whether childhood conditioning plays any part in the way we interpret experiences remains to be understood. But we can go from shame to shame-free in one thought – and that is all it takes. It sounds so simple, and yet at times it is almost impossible to execute. This is because of all the layers of unhelpful and shameful thinking we add on to our experience. There is also an element of victimhood and judgement that perpetuates this thinking.

It is important to note, however, that we need to feel at least *some* sense of shame, for it prevents us from acting in crazy ways.

One of the ways in which I deal with shame with my coaching clients is to work through their core beliefs before we begin setting any goals. No one can make transformational changes when they're weighed down by a sense of shame about their past.

Before you do anything else, recognise how shame shapes your life and what role it takes. Realise how you shame yourself rather than how you are shamed by others. It is easy to make a habit of self-shaming, and this needs to be dealt with before you can move on.

WATCH THE LANGUAGE THAT YOU USE. Statements such as 'That was stupid' and 'You'll never be good enough' are totally unhelpful. Therefore, it is immensely important to create a new language – a language that prevents self-shaming statements from occurring in both your speech and your inner dialogue.

BE MORE CONSCIOUS OF WHO YOU SURROUND YOURSELF WITH. Make sure that you develop friendships with people who do not consistently shame or put you down. It is really important to surround yourself with people who elevate you.

OPERATE IN THE WORLD AS IF YOU MATTER. Treat other people as if they matter, too. This will shift your energy into a higher gear.

The key here is to remember that shame is the flavour that we add to our experiences. This is generally served with a generous portion of suffering and a side order of guilt. Shame is self-imposed, but it doesn't need to be this way.

Be compassionate with yourself after you've gone through a difficult event or experience. Be prepared to succumb to certain feelings of shame or judgement, which are completely understandable, but don't forget to be gentle with yourself. This might be easier said than done, yet it is important to remember that we all make mistakes and we are all trying our best to make our lives as painless as possible.

Life is about making choices. Choose to move towards becoming the victor, not the victim, of an experience, and this will impact all the choices you make from here on. Make the shift in perception allowing you to flavour, spice up or sweeten your experiences in life.

How you approach shame and humiliation is always a matter of perspective; remember that you, and not outside events, shape your inner-experience.

24: Strive to Be a Full-Time Learner

I once met a man who learnt to play the cello at 79 years old. I was mesmerised and drawn to him because of his ability to pursue intellectual stimulation and continue to grow and learn during his so-called autumnal years.

He had previously been a well-respected anaesthetist in a top hospital in Johannesburg, and by now was fully retired. With his extra free time, he wanted a new challenge, goal and purpose as a way of feeling connected, vibrant and living with a sense of aliveness. What wonderful lessons I learnt as I listened to him passionately relating the details of how his newly acquired skill had changed him. It had expanded his world, he said, beyond the stuffy hospital environment he was so used to. I was drawn to his enthusiasm for setting time aside to create something new and different.

This begged the question: when do we stop learning, growing and expanding in the way we did whilst we were children, with all the innate curiosity which invited adventure, exploration and fun?

It's interesting that we spend the first 20 or so years of our lives engaged in learning, studying and being told we have to know more, be more, achieve more. Then suddenly we reach an age where learning is no longer encouraged, admired or celebrated. In its place, we divert our energies to encouraging our children to study, achieve top grades in exams, or become the best player in their school football team. But we put our own self-development under lock and key. Why do we give up exploring our own wants and needs?

People who have reached mid-life (I count myself within this category) often feel there is a need to pack up and suspend their dreams, hopes and aspirations. In some cases, we transfer them to our children, so they can live it out for us instead. But what if we never stopped growing emotionally, psychologically and spiritually? What if we continued to dream, reaching out for what we desire and uncovering more of our true self?

As I watched my teenage daughter set off on her much-anticipated gap year adventure, I wondered why adults don't have a gap year. After all, surely we deserve one more than teenagers do. Other than countless exams, most of them haven't experienced enough stress or broken dreams and expectations. We could benefit from it as a way to regain our bearings and welcome back the person who got lost in other people's expectations. Why don't we take up the activities we never got to learn in our earlier years, such as playing an instrument, taking a dance class, practising sports, volunteering, learning about ourselves or exploring the world?

There is a time to take out the life compass and discover which location we are in. After spending years nurturing a relationship, rearing children, working, caring for elderly parents and facing up to all the responsibilities that life brings, if we reach mid-life virtually unscathed, we deserve a medal. I believe the reward of a mid-life gap year would be extremely welcome – a way to breathe, slow down, and examine what we have spent the last few decades creating. To reflect on whether we're still going in the direction we want to go. To explore the things we never tasted or experienced. It's never too late to reinvent the wheel – or ourselves.

What is stopping you from picking up a new instrument, exploring a different career choice, learning a new hobby or exposing yourself to a different environment? Reawaken yourself, and a more authentic part of you will come to the forefront. This part of you may be ready to play, free of inhibitions, constraints and rules. Instead of the inner parental voice telling you what you can and can't do, this can be swept to one side and silenced once and for all.

As adults, we are free to choose what we want, when we want it. We are free to choose to grow, expand and connect with all the incredible elements that continual learning provides. It brings gifts which have the potential to make us feel alive, excited and energised. Take advantage of that freedom whilst you're still capable of choosing what you want.

25: Feedback Is Crucial

One of the most potent journeys we undertake as human beings is the path towards self-actualisation. As we journey, though, something worms its way into our minds, leading to self-defeating behaviours and stumbling blocks. This is the addictive need for approval, and it inhibits the process of self-discovery and self-actualisation. The preoccupation with others' opinions doesn't allow for this internal growth to happen organically.

As children, we are curious about our world. We don't imagine anyone judging our crawling capabilities or our rocking from side to side in our first attempts to walk. We don't care if food dribbles down our chin. At this point in our development, our intellectual capability is limited, but this is essentially how we start out. We aren't born anxious or stressed, wondering whether the midwife who delivers us thinks we're pretty or a scrunched, wrinkled mass. We came into the world pure and perfect. And, in fact, we still are. There are just layers of unhelpful thoughts, habits and approval-seeking behaviours that have become lodged in our being, getting in the way of further personal progression.

During our early years, as long as our basic human needs are met, we continue with an uncomplicated way of seeing the world. Then something happens that halts the process. There is a before and after.

There was a time when we didn't care what people thought as we played in the playground with our best friend, the way we ran aimlessly in a game of rounders on the beach whilst the sun set in the background, or preoccupied ourselves with our toys, using Lego bricks to create our masterpiece without limitation or shame.

There was no concern with approval or making an impression. We didn't care; we could simply *be*, unashamedly.

Then a situation occurs which communicates we will only be loved and accepted if we toe the line, please everyone and become a good child.

This is where the desire for approval begins, and it is totally conditional. We even get rewarded with shiny stars and sweets when we do this. Approval-seeking grows in size and extends into adulthood, permeating personal relationships, work, entrepreneurship, innovation, and even the articles we dare to write. It spills over the whole panorama of life like a glass of rancid milk which becomes more odorous over time. Before we know it, our life decisions are based on the thought process and the approval of others, which is the only way we think we can fit in.

Think back to your childhood. I'm not reverting back to my psychotherapy days, trying to find the wounded and hurt child. I am looking for the happy child; the one before *that* thought came into play. The thought that told you it wasn't okay to be you.

If the approval-seeking thought wasn't there, how would you express yourself?

There is a primal need we all have for safety, security, protection and belonging. In our desire to belong, feel safe and find security, many of us do whatever we can to seek permission from others before we proceed with anything. I know because I have been at the mercy of this over the years, and have seen others fall into the same trap. After all, to be considered a member of society, we have to toe the line. It's like begging to be allowed into the elite football team when we are in primary school. Everyone wants to be part of something. No one wants to be the outsider.

A few years back, a corporate client told me, 'I can't be too different or expressive in my ideas. It goes against the mould they've set for me.' As with all moulds, once it was set, it turned rock hard and was difficult to break through.

So how can self-actualising and approval seeking co-exist in harmony? They can't.

Approval needs to be replaced by feedback from people we love and respect – those who are growing, developing and doing what we would love to be involved in. Feedback is valuable and facilitates the journey to self-actualisation because it gives us a second set of eyes. Feedback invites possibility and approval invites neediness.

In order to receive feedback, we have to be receptive to what is being offered from someone we trust and hold in high esteem. Feedback is valuable and facilitates the journey to self-actualising. When receiving feedback, our inner stance must be that we are willing to learn, develop, and find new ways of doing things. We better ourselves by asking questions and understanding what is getting in the way of taking the next step into growth. This bears no resemblance whatsoever to the approval seeking stance where we're highly sensitive to how people are reacting to us.

I was working with a client recently who wanted to communicate to his prospects what his business could do for them. He was so deeply into his cognitive thought processes that I felt I would require a crowbar to open him up.

As time went on, this uptight and anxious client began to reveal how he had been a mischievous, curious, fun child. He even detailed a couple of the escapades he had got up to whilst in school.

'Where has this person gone?' I asked.

A difficult family situation had occurred in his early teenage years. He decided then that in order to gain approval, he needed to keep the real part of himself shut away.

'But this is the best part of you,' I told him.

I encouraged him to let his prospects see what a warm yet professional person he was underneath the armour. They would then be far more likely to hire him precisely because he brought a level of humanity into the professional arena. The more he became more authentic, the more he naturally began to attract prospects and clients who fitted in with the kind of projects he really wanted to be involved in. This wasn't about changing him; it was about making him more of who he was.

He was receptive to the feedback, trusted the process and the result spoke for itself.

I could really relate to his experience as approval seeking was one of the biggest struggles I had when I began writing online a number of years ago. My fear was that others wouldn't approve of my opinion; that it may even be met with disapproval or criticism. Then I invited feedback from those I respected and valued as a way of improving my craft whilst holding firmly on to my individuality. As a result of this, I stopped writing articles to impress and fit into a certain dialogue to use as a marketing tool. Instead, now I write what I live and love.

If just one person gets value from my book and it changes the way they view their experiences, then my job is done.

Don't mould yourself to appeal to ideal clients, prospects, groups or niches. Let go of strategy and focus on communicating on an authentic level.

There is a primal need to fit in which sets in during the early years of our life. In commencing adulthood, we step into independence, and part of this process is to have the maturity to decide what we want without looking over our shoulder to see how others will perceive us.

In the same way that we update and reboot our computer regularly, we need to update how we think, act and react in the face of external validation. It's never too late to install a new program that will be of better use in the journey towards growth and self-actualisation.

26: Stop Contemplating

The moment I dread the most each week is when I'm about to hit the cold swimming pool early on a Sunday morning and start my first length. This forces me to muster all my motivation and stamina. By contrast, the following 25 lengths are a breeze and require no effort whatsoever.

Making a start is the hardest part of any journey, whether we are attempting a morning swim or starting a project which requires focus and momentum. This is because we are going from zero to action, from formlessness into form. To start a new mode of behaviour or action, we take ourselves out of our routine. But over time, as this behaviour incrementally becomes routine, we form a new pattern.

Imagine a venture you would like to pursue. What if you could explore and learn as you worked through it? This is not about ploughing blindly into the abyss, hoping and praying that it will all work out, or pouring away money or resources; it is about choosing an activity or project you have always wanted to tackle and doing the first thing required to get it in motion.

Often we stand on the edge of desire, convinced we don't know enough and need more information. So we book more courses, take more notes, log in to more webinars, but the project still stays firmly under wraps. The reality is that lack of information is not the issue, since this is swiftly resolved through a visit to YouTube, Google or Wikipedia. Rather than engaging in contemplation, why not just start, and carry on until you complete?

I remember wanting to write a novel, but waiting for my English grammar to be at almost Shakespearian level. Alongside this, I needed a brilliant idea, and I wanted to know who would buy the book before I even considered sitting down to type the first word. All this made a wonderful excuse to procrastinate.

Then I did something different. I joined National Novel Writing Month, where I was required to write a 50,000 word novel in April. Not a perfect novel, just a first draft created in 30 days. The beauty of this was that it was a totally new experience. It meant no more excuses; the 50,000 words would simply have to be written.

I recall the moment I sat down on 1 April, knowing I had committed to writing a set amount of words each day. Soon, I had a habit of sitting at my desk to write for one hour each morning before I coached my clients, arising an hour earlier than usual in order to fit in the writing. To my utter astonishment, the words filled the pages, which turned into chapters, which transformed into a story that I began to feel connected to. Before I knew it, the 30 days were over and I had written the 50,000 words. It was achieved not through a whole day's work, but one hour each day of focused attention.

During those 30 days, I learnt much about myself through the experience of developing characters emerging from my imagination, creating a plot, changing the dialogue and building new subplots. I had not known how to do this when I started, and in the process I had dropped the need for validation from others. I wrote as a way of expressing what I wanted to share with the world. I had waited long enough to start, but once I did, I committed myself wholeheartedly.

I began to come up with ideas for other projects I could create, which I would never have imagined beforehand. One piece of creativity led to others. It was a process of self-discovery that wouldn't have grown in the midst of a webinar, programme or YouTube video.

If you are an information junkie, but never seem to get started, then you require a different tactic. Just do it, whatever 'it' is for you. It can't be worse than waiting for that perfect moment.

As children, many of us were given a table full of arts and crafts materials and encouraged to unleash our creative ability. However messy we ended up, with hands covered in paint, it was fun. Whatever the outcome of our artwork, the process of picking the colours and deciding which shapes to create was all part of the fun.

Yet then there came a time when we became too scared to get messy; to try things; to play around with what we love and see what we could create. We must relearn how to express ourselves in whichever way we choose and then step back to view it. Each day we have the potential to create, however imperfectly, but most of us wait for the perfect moment which will arrive, we believe, like a convenient sign from above, telling us that *now* is the time to begin. But the secret is simply to take one step at a time in the direction we wish to pursue. If we never do it, it will never happen.

Develop a desire for what you want and take the first step, however small. Then carry on until completion, learning what you need to along the way.

Part Four
RELEASE CONTROL

27: Simplicity of Movement

I have always been a fitness fanatic and was a dancer in my teenage years, having joined nearly every dance class going. What used to attract me was loud music pounding out and excessive movement to ensure a full body workout.

This was until I discovered a different mode of exercise: the yoga session. A stillness and simplicity which I had not experienced before.

The prospect of integrating a gentle and at times static routine into my fitness regime would have made my anxiety rise a number of years ago. I would have complained that the actions and movements were too slow, and frankly it would have made me itch to run out the door.

A while back, I was experiencing challenging personal issues and juggling a tough legal situation. I was finding it difficult to focus on an end result, and decision making was becoming tough. I knew I needed to approach my problem from a different angle. Joining a yoga course was one of the best decisions I made during this time.

Yoga is becoming more popular each day. It is not uncommon to observe a business-savvy man or woman sprint out of the office, yoga mat in hand, ready for the next instalment of this brilliant discipline. The reality is that stressed businesspeople or entrepreneurs run the risk of making bad decisions or settling on wrong choices due to an overly busy mind. You don't have to be bohemian or deeply into spirituality to reap the benefits of yoga – it is about settling your mind and body and becoming more connected. Yoga practice helped me navigate my life in such simple, but powerful ways. This discipline was important in ensuring that the decisions I was making came from a calm place.

GROUNDING YOURSELF BEFORE YOU START. Yoga practice commences with your eyes closed, deep breathing and connecting to your inner core. The outside world is somehow shut away. This ensures that as you get into different yoga positions, you are approaching them from your inner core with good intentions.

I can't tell you how chaotic and uncertain life was in my outside world when I took up this discipline, but it kept my inner world stable and intact.

KEEP YOUR EYE ON AN OBJECT AND FOCUS. When you're attempting yoga positions, often others around you will be wobbling and trying to stay balanced. If you focus on them, you will also lose your balance and fall. Shut all distractions out and focus on one static object in the room.

This was absolutely key for me. I had to stop getting distracted by all the superficiality, and the people who were diverting me from staying 'on course'. Yoga taught me to anchor myself and focus on my end goal, shutting out the external voices that had the potential to contaminate my decisions.

YOU ARE CAPABLE OF FAR MORE THAN YOU IMAGINE. When I originally started yoga, I feared how far I could push my body as some of the positions were extremely challenging. The biggest surprise was that the more I stretched and pushed beyond what I thought I could manage, the more my body adapted to this (as long as it wasn't physically painful). This didn't just push me out of my physical comfort zone, but also my emotional one. Whenever I thought I was only capable of stretching my body up to a certain point, I found that point extended each time I attempted it. This encouraged me to reach for far more in life than I ever thought I could and to push the limits of my capability.

AT TIMES WE JUST NEED A SLIGHT TWEAK FOR CHANGES TO OCCUR. When you're mastering yoga postures, there are certain ways you are encouraged to breathe and hold your body. Once you are in position, the yoga instructor may need to nudge and tweak certain parts of your body to get you into alignment. These nudges and tweaks are very subtle.

There are times in life when you don't need to make huge transformations, just slight shifts in your thinking, habits or behaviour patterns. This can make all the difference and produce tremendous results.

LISTEN TO YOUR BODY. The body is an incredible mechanism with the gift of insights and wisdom that nothing else can produce. Listen to it. If your body is in pain when you are getting into position, then stop immediately.

This is key in yoga, and in life generally. Listen to your body if you're stressed or anxious, or if something doesn't feel right. The way the body communicates the need to stop is your inbuilt guide to life.

The rewards I reaped from yoga sessions were multiple. It inspired me to succeed throughout the situation I was facing by sharpening my focus, determination and tenacity at a pretty chaotic time. This meant that all the decisions I made felt right and came from a stress free and effortless mindset.

It is mind blowing how much you can achieve and how creative you can get when your mind becomes still and relaxed. If you yearn for more achievement and creativity in your life, I highly recommend you try out this discipline which can be traced back 5,000 years. At times, we have to reach out for the wisdom of the past to resolve the issues of the present, and yoga's long, rich history is proof of this.

28: Take the Overwhelm Out of Change

We are incredible beings with a talent for multi-tasking. We are capable of running the home, relationships, personal life and business life simultaneously. But there's one thing pretty much all of us are wildly guilty of, and this is procrastinating – making excuses and leaving aspirations on the back-burner for that ever distant 'some day'.

Excuses can take on a life of their own. You may say, 'I'll follow my dreams once the kids leave home', 'Once I'm more financially secure', 'When my partner requires less of me'. The list goes on. But here's the thing: what if you could kick-start your life or business, regardless of kids, partners or money issues, right now? Even though it might be years after you said you would expand your business, write that book, start public speaking, or take up a new hobby.

Now, I'm not asking you to throw in the towel, abandon your home and live in an ashram in India. This kind of thinking is a problem, for any change that we imagine doing in the future can easily become distorted and take on overwhelming proportions. What seemed like a good idea initially suddenly becomes our worst case scenario. No wonder we procrastinate and fail to act.

What if you could start with the small things? Not everything is about making a huge change overnight. I believe that most changes happen over time. By paying daily attention to what you want, you can create the incremental changes you desire. It simply starts with taking action, however small.

Many people feel overwhelmed each time they reflect on their five or ten year plan. It's heavy, locked-in and lacks creativity, flow and movement. The way to overcome this is to focus on this week. One week at a time, a new life is created. This stops us feeling overwhelmed by the weight of having to keep to a larger plan. Who knows, in any event, what opportunities may come to us in six months and what we might have to overcome during this time?

It is important, however, to examine the terrain from the outset. Tell the truth about where your life currently stands. This is the only way that you can get from where you are now to where you want to be.

Ask yourself, 'Which aspect of my life or business is crying out for change? What could I be doing differently?

'What would this do for me? And what would be the best part?'

Be as specific as you can and keep refining it.

'What impact does this have on other areas of life? And if I could let go of the thinking that stops me, what would life look like?'

There are a few areas to become more aligned with:

YOUR BODY. From the moment you awaken, get your body and your spirit in motion. Practise gratitude and visualise what you'll create that day, as this will teach you the art of leadership. I go for a run, power walk, or even dance in the morning if it's raining (British weather has encouraged me to be more creative). The aim is to get your body out of a stagnant and hopeless place and into movement, fun and possibility.

YOUR LANGUAGE. The words you use to speak about your life or explain your stories often show your limiting beliefs. You need to tell a different story using different words, using the language of expansion and possibility. Notice when you use words such as 'should', 'must', 'need', 'have to' – these are words that generally carry a demand with them. Begin to swap these for the words 'choose' or 'don't choose to'. Change your words; change your life story.

YOUR FOCUS. What you focus on becomes your perceived reality – the lens you look through. For example, if you really wanted a white Mini Cooper, I can assure you that everywhere you looked, everyone would seem to have one. Suddenly you begin to notice what you've up till then disregarded. Mindset works in the same way. If you have a negative mindset, negativity is all you will see.

Life is about progression, growing and being more of who you are so you can effectively serve others. Procrastinating and holding back pull you away from sharing the best of who you are and what you could offer to the world.

Marianne Williamson encapsulates this beautifully when she says, 'Our deepest fear is not that we are inadequate. Our deepest fear is that we are powerful beyond measure.'

Let go of any excuses that are holding you back. This may actually be the time to step into who you were meant to be.

29: Time Is of the Essence

T ime travel is not just an extraordinary concept reserved for the 1980s movie *Back to the Future*. In fact, it became real to me a number of weeks ago as I travelled overseas.

After undergoing 11 hours on a flight from London to Arizona, I was quite pleased with the fact that since the time at my destination was eight hours behind the UK, I would be able to relive that amount of time. The universe had kindly gifted me an extra eight hours that day.

This raised the question: what if we could all relive eight hours each day? What would we change? What would be different and why? What would we skim away and what would we hold on to?

In my culture, we recite a short blessing each morning as we awaken, where we give thanks to God (for some, it may be another higher power, the universe or energy) for having returned our soul to us, clean and ready to start anew. This blessing gives us the chance to forgive the past and let it go, and approach the day with renewed energy and anticipation of what we can create without being weighed down with yesterday's issues or mistakes.

Many people don't see it as critical that they start what they intend to do; they just take time for granted. They procrastinate, complain, expect, but they don't see that each day brings a new dawn, a renewal and a chance to use time with added vigour.

The co-founder of Apple Computers, Steve Jobs, used to ask himself each morning, 'If today were the last day of my life, would I want to do what I'm about to do today? If the answer is 'no' for too many days in a row, I know I need to change something.' I'm not trying to encourage morbid thoughts of death, but imagine how quickly you would develop any projects waiting in the pipeline if you lived life as if your time was truly finite. Which of course it is.

Most of us want to make a difference, impact others in some positive way, but the issue is that we don't know how to use time. We waste it unnecessarily on distractions, checking our e-mails constantly, engaging in unnecessary Facebook activity, or posting and reposting on social media to gain some external validation. We might even spend it on people who drain our energy.

The late singer and songwriter George Michael – whose death had quite an impact on my life, for his song writing carried a depth that I felt but could not put into words – summed this up for me in one of my favourite songs, 'Playing For Time'. After his death, this song held a whole new meaning for me. I had first heard it in my 30s as a new mother, and it held a particular poignancy back then. Over two decades later, it has opened into something altogether different and much more meaningful. It signals our need to make endless excuses which keep us stuck where we are.

The more distractions we have, the further we are from claiming our destiny. We cease to focus on what we need to be doing. This might translate into dysfunctional relationships, dead-end jobs or mindless pursuits. Once we shut out all activities which drain our precious resources, we are then able to focus our time and use it wisely.

It is up to you to become a master of living and working purposefully. It's critical that you gravitate towards aligning your strengths, passions and goals so that life doesn't pass you by.

30: Simplify Your Life

Have you ever overindulged in a meal to the point you're unable to take another bite? Something similar happened to me a short while ago, although I had not eaten the entire contents of my overstocked fridge until I was at bursting point. Instead, I had taken on an excessive number of projects. As a result of this, I felt exhausted, overwhelmed and drained. For days, it was as if I were lugging around a suitcase of heavy glassware, scared that at any moment I would drop it and break its contents into a million tiny fragments.

This is when one powerful insight jumped into my awareness whilst I was walking my dog on a cold, blustery afternoon in London. As I walked aimlessly through the foliage on Hampstead Heath, I found myself simply admiring the scenery right in front of my eyes. I then added to this peaceful moment by turning off my phone.

I had come across a powerful but calm shift of mindset; the answer to why I had been dragging my feet for the past few days. The answer I received from the universe was simple: I was suffering from pure, unadulterated exhaustion.

I had a vision of being full to capacity and someone offering me another spoonful of food. As much as I might try to open my mouth, I would be incapable of taking one tiny bite. That was exactly what life felt like back then. Just as our stomachs automatically inform us when to stop eating, so our minds can warn us that we are too full of psychological and emotional contents. I was full to the brim and could no longer consume any more.

I decided in that moment that the only thing for me to do was to stop. I had to look around and examine the commitments I had 'eaten', so to speak, in the past few months. It was like doing a mental inventory of the food I consume when beginning a diet. The first thing I'd do is to create a food diary to see where the calories were coming from.

So I created a life diary. As I sat down and catalogued all the things I had done in the past few months, I was astonished at what was occupying most of my days. I had travelled extensively, including long haul flights to seven different countries. I was also writing articles, dealing with personal and family life, honouring speaking engagements, and undertaking a specialised programme in America. All whilst, of course, continuing to coach my wonderful clients. Was it any wonder I could barely move? I had in fact depleted my resources.

As I stared at what was in front of me, I realised I had to cut out the emotional 'fats', 'carbohydrates' and 'sugars'. Ruthlessly, I cut out what was not serving me, what I was emotionally allergic to, skimming away actions, tasks, activities and things that overwhelmed me. This was liberating; a way of purging all that was unnecessary. It felt *so* good.

We don't notice how busy we are, bingeing on projects or ventures we think will give us a momentary fix or joy. In reality, each project, action or responsibility piles up the 'life calories', leading to extra weight which makes it difficult to be productive. In our desire to change the world, sometimes we take on too much.

It was important that I digested what I had experienced before rushing off to the next venture or action. The wonderful thing about my insight was that the minute I became aware of what was happening, a feeling of calm enveloped me. I knew in my gut what the solution was, and there was simplicity about it: I put some of the activities and tasks on hold for three months. This would give me time to digest everything I had done and allow it to enter my system, whilst I learnt precious lessons along the way.

I'm currently feeling as light as a feather. In following my 'life diet', I feel as if I've lost a couple of stone already. I didn't need to cure procrastination or turn up my productivity; I just needed to cut away the things that were depleting my resources, draining my energy and simply not serving me.

If you're feeling stressed or overwhelmed, ask yourself one simple question: What are the extra 'life calories' you could cut out?

31: Create a Freedom Mindset

In parts of south east Asia, young elephants are mercilessly tied to a rope to keep them in a confined area as a method of conditioning. As the elephants grow and develop in size, they believe they can't break free. Even when the rope has been removed, they still proceed to stay firmly within their limited area. Adult elephants can reach a weight of up to 14,000 pounds and can tower over 13 feet tall, yet they never leave the confines preset by their master in their formative years.

Although we don't resemble this pachyderm in size or intellectual capacity, we still chain ourselves to certain concepts, ideas and limitations set by others, and then live them.

Ask yourself in relation to your life: Are you keeping within the confines of an imaginary boundary, too scared to venture out beyond what you've become accustomed to? The key to escaping is to retrain the mind to let go of self-imposed limitations. With a limited mindset, preconceived decisions dictate actions, and venturing out of this can seem impossible.

The elephant is one of the largest and most powerful animals on Earth. Its true calling is to lead, nurture and protect. We too have our own precious destiny waiting. And it will continue to wait until we're ready to step out of the claustrophobic confines that have been set by our master. That master is our own mind on an unconscious level.

Those who fear venturing further afield will not risk finding themselves out of control, out of their measured safe zone. Like ploughing through a thick, dark forest after nightfall, they find it frightening to be in unfamiliar territory. But limited thought creates a limited life, lived on a never-ending vague quest for something that'll be out there one day. Except there is nothing out there to run to. Freedom is not to be grasped and captured; it's a mindset we all have access to.

There are a number of ways to attain true freedom in all its many forms. We need to be psychologically independent of all subjugation, servitude and powers that demean value. This requires a certain freedom of the spirit. The soul is not free if it is subjected to demands that prevent it from following its inner truth. This control is mostly imaginary.

We are truly free when we're faithful to the truth of who we are. This allows us to effortlessly live a fulfilled life which is focused on the soul's inner goals. Those whose spirit is servile to external and internal limitations will never experience this sense of self-fulfilment. Their happiness will always depend upon outside factors.

The powerful elephant must be rehabilitated in a sanctuary to begin the process of ridding itself of the limits imposed by the rope around its leg. We must similarly rid ourselves of the rope tied around our lives that keeps us exactly where we are: static and too scared to move forward. But unlike the captive elephant who requires a human to set it free, we can set ourselves free by taking a small step out of the confines we have set for ourselves, thus becoming who we were meant to be. Without limits.

32: Don't Chase Success

Some time ago, I received one of the most incredible proposals I have had so far. It was from a producer in Los Angeles who wanted to discuss an article I had written about divorce. This particular article had been floating around on various writing platforms online until it was picked up by this producer. They were intrigued by the person who had written it and wanted to find out more about me.

We scheduled a meeting to speak further via Skype. It felt strange to be sitting in my living room in London on a cold winter's night, speaking to a production manager who was basking in the afternoon sunshine in Los Angeles whilst sipping on her latte. The moment was totally surreal, but the proposal, although attractive and potentially lucrative, was not something I was willing to consider, even though it could have catapulted me on to a global platform and ensured my success.

The whole process provided a number of important lessons. When writing the article, I wasn't fully aware of whether I was targeting a niche or a wider audience. I wrote from my heart with zero expectation, and had no idea it would be picked up by a producer in Los Angeles a number of years later. I simply wrote using my authenticity.

It irks me when I consistently see adverts and promotions as a way of making a quick buck. Earning six and seven figures in a short space of time is the way to do things these days. The sense of real value has evaporated. It seems as if people want to pick up Willy Wonka's golden ticket. Or, in more recent times, Justin Bieber's YouTube video which catapulted him to success when it went viral in a very short amount of time.

In the old days, we had artisans and apprentices who spent years mastering a craft. They learnt from the leaders in their field, and then went out into the world, practising constantly as they mastered their art whilst growing their experience and knowledge. This is so unlike the urgency that I see today, where people are incapable of slowing down and navigating the process of pain, rejection and failure. We are bombarded by messages on social media telling us we can write a book in five days, set up a coaching practice in a fortnight, or run an online business with a six figure income within the first month. Financial freedom beckons, and this financial freedom will eliminate worries and propel us into the life we dream about. But no one wants to endure the often treacherous journey to get there.

I see it constantly in those I encounter. They want to create a business – and it'd better be fast. They want to find their life's purpose real quick. They want to find their niche now. They want to bypass the agony of being patient and waiting.

It seems we have to know it all and we have to achieve it all now.

There is then an attempt to jettison an uncomfortable feeling brewing inside, which often translates into uncertainty and anxiety about the unknown. This makes it difficult to slow down and listen to what the one next step needs to be.

The reality is that those who spend years slowly but surely building and perfecting their craft out of devotion stand out. Their message is consistent, contains value and shows they have identified and conquered uncertainty and anxiety. They've made mistakes, fallen flat on their faces at times, but they've kept going. They've mastered their strengths, and this shows in every fibre of their being.

The main ingredient to achieving success is a commitment that we will do whatever we set out to do, no matter how long it takes. I'm aware that this can waiver with a lack of belief in our capabilities. At times, it feels like the treacherous journey in *The Hobbit* as we experience one obstacle after another. We imagine metaphorical dragons, goblins and sorcerers, but there are also wizards and magic. We have to create the magic as we navigate this journey.

The artist Vincent Van Gogh spent years learning his art, copying the masters and perfecting his brush strokes. His art changed direction a number of times. He explored and tested different portraits as well as painting on different textures of canvas. He lived in different places to try out the ambience on his painting style. As time went on, he developed his own artistic flair. He didn't become an artist in a year with a seven figure salary, and we can learn so much from this.

Everything that is created has a process of slowly filtering through, so the results are not immediate. That's not to say that the people we would like to attract aren't noticing or acknowledging us; they are simply building a relationship of trust with us, and this also takes time.

It would be more productive if individuals spent less time chasing and more time slowing down and gaining clarity as to what they really want. Through learning where their strengths lie and how they can make even the smallest impact, they would be far more satisfied than those chasing the ever-receding finishing line of success like an Olympic runner. The way to do this is to take success out of the equation. In this way, we focus on serving, on speaking our truth, on making a difference as we proceed and find our own unique platform. Before we know it, success lands on our shoulder like a butterfly trying to attract attention. But we have to let success happen by not following it. In the long run, success will follow us.

Slow down and turn off the outside noise. Turn inwards and discover what you truly want, what difference you can make (however small), and how you would like to serve your audience and your tribe. In fact, care so much about what you want to communicate that you stop caring about impressing, convincing or cajoling anyone. Do it with intention and love.

33: Create Commitments

One of the best productivity tools I have ever used is the 80/20 Rule, which is also known as the Pareto Principle after the Italian economist, Vilfredo Pareto. The Pareto Principle invites us to focus on the 20% of our actions which create 80% of our results. It was a revelation to discover what percentage of my day was dedicated to activities that either achieved my desired results or distanced me from them.

This method outweighs all the goal setting I previously spent time crafting, and all the other systems I was engaged in to keep me on track. It is far more effective, for example, than those dreaded New Year's resolutions.

Everything looks great on paper – especially goals, outcomes and results, but usually we haven't got a backup plan for when distractions get in the way; or those moments when we're pulled in a million different directions and our desire to be involved stretches us to the limit.

A while back, I was coaching a self-employed website designer who wanted to expand his business. He had invested in expensive courses and training to get him on track, but nothing seemed to work. He mainly struggled with productivity in the morning as his mobile phone was his alarm clock. As soon as the alarm sounded, he would pick it up and take the opportunity to scroll through various social media sites. Before he knew it, it was 11am, and by then he'd lost interest and did not feel inspired to do any work.

I suggested an extremely simple solution. It's mind blowing how the simplest tweaks often work far better than complexity. I asked him to invest in an old-fashioned alarm clock and keep the phone out of the bedroom. As the distraction was the phone, it needed to be eliminated from his morning routine.

An alarm clock will get you out of bed in the morning, but there is a deeper question that needs asking. What are you committed to? If it's staying in bed until 11am, then own it. But if you're committed to something more, then you have to erase everything that is getting in the way. This presents an extra challenge if you're self-employed. There is no longer a boss keeping you on your toes, someone you need to check in with at 9am sharp. There is simply you at the mercy of how you feel on that day. If you don't feel inspired, scroll through your phone for a while, skip a few hours and take the afternoon off. If you feel great, work until late evening, cancelling dinner plans on your way. It becomes a case of either 'I feel like it' or 'I don't feel like it.'

I'm not saying dismiss your feelings as they are important and should be acknowledged. But you need to develop a desire for what you want and gain a degree of clarity on what is important to you. It isn't about being selfish or narcissistic; it's about leading a life in a more conscious way. Make choices rather than being sucked into everything that is happening externally.

A coaching client of mine had a tendency to arrive late. I didn't want to sit in judgement; I just sat in curiosity. What was getting in the way of this client arriving on time? More importantly, what did it say about his world? We had both agreed to show up on time for our sessions, but now he was at the mercy of life, guilt and people pleasing. It was clear he felt compelled to say yes to everyone else's requests, which made him late, unreliable and unproductive.

What's wrong with telling people we're simply not available? We need to take ownership of how we're using time. If we're saying yes to one thing, we are saying no to something else. It's a simple equation.

Imagine being a warrior fighting to enter a castle to reach an overflowing pot of gold which is hidden deep inside. There is an army standing in the way, and you have to slay everyone who stops you from entering the castle. You can't stand there dithering and playing with the marigolds in the field.

Distraction is one of the biggest enemies of creating the results we want. I know this because I was seduced by its power in the past. You only had to show me a shiny object and I would follow it blindly, and if the Pied Piper of Hamelin had played his tune, I probably would have followed him too. Every so often I'm still drawn by distractions, but I now recognise that it's a form of avoidance.

Distractions have some luxurious and inviting qualities. These can be heavily disguised as networking events, long, drawn-out coffee mornings with connections, toxic relationships, social media sites, or they can be as simple as being available to everyone at any time.

Observe where your energy hangs out during the day. Is it at the mercy of every e-mail, phone call or text which pings into your phone whilst you're in the middle of a project? This constant availability and being involved in everything, often because of a desire to feel needed, is the biggest killer of workflow and productivity.

One of the things the Pareto Principle taught me was that I could erase everything that wasn't bringing anything to the table, and further eliminate whatever was draining my energy. In doing this, I skimmed away more than half of my activities, focusing only on what was in line with what I wanted. Everything else had to go. There was a certain ruthlessness about it. Like the warrior, I slayed all the distractions that were time-consuming, senseless and pointless. And there were plenty.

What helped me do this initially was to have an activity log. In the log, I kept a note of what I did each day. After two weeks, this allowed me to see clearly what I was busy (or not busy) doing every day. It made for insightful reading.

My day doesn't need to be all about action, for it is key that I have space to reflect and use as a creativity tool. In fact, allowing space within the day is as important as breathing. It's where the magic happens, and it's miles better than being excessively busy or committed to things I may not even want to be doing. Where I had to develop mastery was in distinguishing which space was a creative one, and which was a pure distraction.

I ask myself regularly: what's the best use of this moment? If it is knuckling down to completing what needs to be done, then I complete it. If the best use of my time is to take time out because I feel overwhelmed or to engage creativity, then that's what I choose to do.

Just after a terrorist attack in the UK recently, I was meant to travel by tube to the West End for an event that I had been looking forward to attending and that marked the next stage in my business. I'm not an anxious person by nature, but I felt more than a little nervous stepping into the train carriage. I was well aware that I would spend my time sitting in my seat, uncomfortably assessing each person who walked past, especially if they were holding a bag larger than a clutch purse. But the event was a talk given by a well-known publishing house I wanted to approach and no terrorist threat was going to stop me from attending.

This reminded me that we need to renew our internal commitments regularly, questioning how much we want each one rather than blindly pushing ourselves to be motivated. In recent times, I have seen a trend for married couples to renew their vows as a way of strengthening the commitment they made to each other all those years ago. I believe we need to do something similar with our business and personal lives. Let's renew our vows to ourselves as a reminder of what we're committed to, and become increasingly masterful at declining what doesn't fit with this.

The Florentine sculptor Michelangelo was given a huge block of marble stone with the expectation that it would be turned into a work of art. He worked solidly for two years, removing all that was unnecessary to create the magnificent statue of David. I'm sure there were times when Michelangelo was tired, unmotivated and couldn't bear to see another piece of stone, but he was committed to the result.

In life, we're given a block of time, and it's up to us to shape the hours and days, persistently chipping away and eliminating all that is unnecessary and gets in the way of what we want.

34: Overthinking Versus Doing

After a trip abroad which included vast amounts of airline delays and cancellations, I was given the opportunity to claim a hefty compensation. All I needed to do was to complete a compensation form and send off to the airline company. Yet it sat in my office for weeks after we had returned from our holiday, because I had so many paralysing thoughts about completing it.

The thought storm included the following favourites from my playlist: 'They will never take my claim seriously', 'Who am I to claim against a global airline?', 'It is my word against theirs'. (I had to prove the extent of the delay.)

You get the picture. You may have your own favourite thoughts that sabotage any action you need to take. My own personal thoughts were so convincing that I made the mistake of searching online for the percentage of people who get compensation from airlines, and the figures were pretty grim. Over the days, I told myself that I'd fill the form in when I had time; when I was not too busy. It took me exactly six weeks to get round to completing it (an activity which took an hour at most to do).

Fewer than ten hours after I had sent the paperwork off in the post, a news report announced that the airline company had gone bust. Had I completed the form earlier on, the compensation would have been safely nestled in my account – as it was for a number of other passengers who claimed immediately after the delayed flights.

The overthinking and questioning myself was a time-consuming exercise which had no benefit, other than to teach me a valuable lesson: today is all we have. Putting things off for later, someday, one day is simply pointless, because they just don't get done. More importantly, nothing is here for ever. We need to seize each moment with both hands. But often we're just too busy doing nothing at all. A busy mind is often a mask for avoidance.

Most of us have 'To do' lists, right? How about a 'Not to do' list – I have to credit my previous coach with bringing this phrase to life for me. If my 'Not to do' list comprises of not doubting myself, not waiting for the opportune moment, not procrastinating and not being at the mercy of people pleasing, surely there will then be time to complete my 'To do' list with full focus.

How many times have you wanted to do something, but have postponed it with no real commitment to when it will be done? It's simply pushed to one side for that 'perfect' moment. But if today was all the time you had left, what would you be engaged in? What would happen to the overthinking that normally plagues your day? There would simply be no time to nurture it, so you'd likely make time for what's important.

We need to get to the core of what stops us from doing what we want, stripping it down.

So what are you overthinking? There is always one thought in the overthinking playlist which shouts louder than the rest. You will know which one it is as it continues to be the stumbling block between you and what you want. The thought could be 'I'm not good enough', which means you're running around trying to prove yourself, or old favourites such as 'I must keep up appearances' or 'no one likes me'.

Slow down and reflect on this one thought.

Author of 'Loving What Is' Byron Katie poses a simple yet powerful question which I often ask my clients when I coach them. She asks, Who would you be without that thought? Like cleaning the cobwebs out of the attic, this is the time to do a clean-up of what goes on in your mind.

Most people feel that analysing these thoughts is the answer, yet all this does is hold the thoughts in place and make them real. Just because a negative thought comes into your mind, it doesn't mean you have to sit it down and make it a cup of tea. Remember that the longer you leave the teabag in, the stronger the tea becomes. It's the same with thinking.

Yet you're always a thought away from experiencing life differently.

I remember coaching a successful businesswoman a while back. At work, she had a pattern of achieving amazing success at the very beginning of a job, and then she would stop. Her initial achievements happened so fast that by the time she reached the first hurdle, she was completely exhausted and burnt out. There was no real flow in the way she approached her work and progression within it. Whilst all her colleagues would continue up the career path at a more consistent pace, she would run past them initially, then get stuck. It was like she'd put all her energy into the first stage of a marathon, then felt exhausted and unable to take another step.

This pattern had been consistent throughout her life because her persistent thoughts were 'I'm not enough' and 'I need to prove myself'. She was certainly proving herself, but it was all being driven by stress and anxiety. She was overthinking it, and not only was this not working, but it was also not enjoyable.

I asked her, 'Who were you before those thoughts came into play?'

Her face softened, she smiled cheekily and told me what a fun person she used to be. It was almost as if she was speaking about a person she used to know who had now disappeared into the distance.

My task was to tease this person out – her real self, before 'I'm not enough' filtered through. We explored what it would be like to add 1% more fun into her business, bringing more of her real self into the equation. She smiled; it was an exciting prospect.

She lived in Malta, so I asked her to take a few hours off, go jet skiing, dancing, maybe even take a class in paddle surfing, rediscovering the fun part of her which had been hidden behind the vast amount of overthinking. If she started to show up from a fun, light and relaxed state, she would model this behaviour to her team.

As time went on and she began to incorporate more fun into her life, she noticed that she felt more relaxed and was running from a different engine. The overthinking had been replaced by fun moments, and the resultant lightness brought about creativity, possibility and laughter – a great recipe for a successful business mindset.

I'm not sure why people believe that work has to be serious, dark, and complex. It's no wonder people look so miserable on the London Underground station at 8.30am. Look at those dour faces, hiding behind either the *Metro* newspaper or their phones, playing a variety of games to keep their mind reaching for something, anything.

Let's observe Google, one of the most successful multinational technology companies. You may imagine Google's workspace to be stuffy, since technology doesn't conjure up an image of fun, laughter or play. However, Google's offices around the world reflect its philosophy, which is nothing less than 'To create the happiest, most productive workplace in the world'. When walking through the Google office or campus, you can find play areas, coffee shops, open kitchens, terraces with chaises longues, and conversation areas designed to look like vintage cars – so one of the most successful companies in the world uses fun rather than encouraging its employees to be serious or overthink their way into success.

This isn't about pushing positive psychology or always being happy; it's simply owning the fact that we're constantly living our thinking, which impacts everything we do and how we interact with the world – whether we're claiming compensation from an airline or doing something far more serious. Since we live in a thought-created reality, our reaction will always be determined by our interpretation of a situation, leading us on to the next action we take.

35: Confront Stress

I t might surprise you to know that a life coach can fall into the stress trap, but stress often enters my world. It all begins with an accumulation of experiences, spiced up with a selection of badly chosen thoughts that I hang on to.

Stress, for those lucky individuals who have not been visited by it, is a dark cloud that takes us over, converting everything in its path into turmoil. We then become a human tornado. The thoughts playing out in the back office of our minds take centre stage, and suddenly what felt manageable seems insurmountable. Stress makes everything seem like an emergency, and no-one performs well when tense – no leader, performer, athlete or parent. When we're in this state, we only have access to a small percentage of our skill and intelligence. This is because our mind is crammed with emotions like expectation, frustration and anger.

And that's just the tip of the iceberg. Then we develop stress for others too – expectations of how they need to behave. So this feeling becomes magnified and we sit in a thick, dark cloud for hours, days or even weeks.

Ask yourself, What is my personal stressor? It's important to recognise it. Is it a person, a recurring situation or something you're trying to avoid?

There is often a circularity to the way we deal with life. Usually, events follow a regular pattern, and although this can be deeply uncomfortable, it is equally comfortable due to its familiarity. But we could step out of the circularity of our stressful thinking as if we're stepping out of a hula hoop.

Often when I ask someone why they feel stressed, they proceed to list all the things they're currently involved with. But busyness does not always equal stress. Busyness is just that: being busy. Being involved with a load of tasks that need doing doesn't in itself cause stress. What does cause stress is having a busy mind. We can have a mountain of tasks we are involved with, and in the mix we include judgements on how each task needs to be performed. I have known women with large families, juggling kids and a multitude of jobs, who have been less stressed than single friends who feel stressed just by adding two more tasks to their 'to do' list.

A great mentor of mine posed an interesting question to me: 'If a drunk person walked towards you in the middle of the road, trying to engage you in conversation, would you stop, listen and take anything they said seriously?'

My answer was, 'Of course not.' Images of the local drunk in my hometown of Gibraltar came to mind. I flinched at the thought of this man with his greasy hair, staggering from side to side, swigging from a bottle of beer. He was to be avoided at all costs.

My mentor continued, 'That's exactly what your thoughts are at times: drunk.'

This was a great way for me to get a sense of how we take our thoughts seriously, getting lost in an *Alice in Wonderland* world, where one moment things look enormous and the next they're tiny again. The accumulation of thoughts which manifest as 'I should', 'I have to', 'I must' brings with it stress of monumental proportions. It has us running around in circles at times.

Of course, not all thoughts are drunk. But we can recognise which ones are because we'll feel great one moment, and then suddenly find ourselves being pulled into a whirlpool of negative emotion. It sucks us right in whilst we hang on for dear life.

What if stress could be confronted rather than suppressed? Rather than feeling as if we need to show it the back door, we could just *be* with it?

Stress is the way our body informs us that we are currently overloaded. In the same way my MacBook Air refuses to work when I have ten different applications open at once, stress tells us we're up to our limit. We have unlimited potential, but we have a limited ability to contain an overload of demands in our mind.

I'm not a Zen master with a cheesy smile who can perfect a yoga pose and chant to the heavens. I have my moments. Yet what I've got better at doing is recognising when the cloud of stressful thinking is about to descend – or has already taken hold in my mind. At that point I know I'm dealing with an intoxicated mind (and I'm teetotal) and I will feel stressed for a while, but I don't ever make decisions from this place. I've learnt not to because my worst decisions have been made from this state.

Thick clouds in the sky block any ray of sunshine being able to come forth, and our thinking works in the same way. Thinking creates our feeling, which creates our experiences moment to moment. We know this is true because five people can have exactly the same tragedy happen to them, but each one will experience it differently, simply because they are at the mercy of what colour or flavour their thinking will add to the overall story.

You can create a Hollywood movie out of thought – it could be *Gone With the Wind* or *Silence of the Lambs*. Your choice. Just never make a serious, life-changing decision from this place.

I know it's often easier said than done. I can only share what I do, and it's not a trip to a psychologist or psychiatrist, although my personal coach can be amazing to talk to at times like these. What helps me is either to navigate through stressful thought until it goes away, or to do something far more fun.

I drive to an English tea shop in the heart of London. It's as authentic as you can get: old fashioned music playing on a small transistor radio; pretty flowered tablecloths; china crockery (not drab cardboard cups); and the best scones and tea delivered with the warmest, friendliest smile. There are no large flat screen televisions blaring out Sky Sports, or people on their phones or laptops, as there is no Wi-Fi or internet connection available. It's just a calm reminder of how life used to be before we became addicted to being busy.

The last time I felt the need to drive there, I picked up a pen and wrote this chapter on a serviette. I had not gone to the tea shop with any intention of writing; I was simply taking some time out. Twenty minutes earlier, I couldn't have written my name, but when my thoughts organically shifted, the words for this chapter came tumbling out. By the time I had devoured the last crumb of scone, the world looked totally different. Nothing had changed externally, but my internal world had, and that's the only thing that matters. I was experiencing the same situations differently. By the time I reached home, I was full of life and ready to tackle whatever came along.

Sometimes I don't even have to go anywhere for the stress to pass, but it's more fun to do so. If I'm feeling stressed, I may as well enjoy the ride.

As a Coach, my daily wellbeing is crucial. I strive to be in a clear state of mind to facilitate my clients' progression, so I'm always mindful of returning to this state of mind, however many times I'm pulled away from it.

Ignoring stressful feelings or pushing them away is impossible, in the same way we can't push the clouds away. We have to wait until the conditions in the atmosphere change, and then the clouds will organically move to reveal the sun, bringing light and clarity. There's nothing we need to do.

Once our thinking moves, we can see clearly, and the path reveals what we need to do next. It sounds simplistic, and on some level, we might require it to have more complexity, but stress is a thermometer of life. It's our body informing us that we're at the mercy of stressful thinking, and, as with any fine instrument, we need to pay attention to it.

Conclusion

As we conclude, my recommendation to you is to take the first step into living more intuitively and authentically.

The learning curve in this book entails looking inside yourself more, and this takes courage, tenacity and vision, but the results will astonish you.

When I work with a client, one of the questions I ask them as our session comes to an end is, 'What's your take away from the session?'

I want to ask you the same question. What are you taking away from this book? If there is anything that inspired you or any insights you had, now would be the perfect time to do something different, and watch what happens as a result. Don't just trust my words; test them, and feel free to share the results with me. I would love to know.

Thank you for giving me the opportunity to share this book with you.

Acknowledgements

I want to acknowledge the following people, who have been so important throughout my life:

My wonderful parents, who are a constant source of inspiration, and my siblings Levi, Delia, Isaac, Victoria and Samuel for being my best mode of support, and my biggest cheerleaders throughout life. To my incredible extended family and friends, who made my childhood in Gibraltar the most magical period of my life.

To the champion coach J.P. Morgan, for encouraging me to spend nine months 'birthing a book' – this was a profound shift for me. The concept of mothering and nurturing a book was all I needed to get started; procrastination and writer's block abandoned me at that precise moment and have not returned.

To all the coaches, consultants, practitioners, mentors and supervisors I have had the honor of working with in the past few years. Each one taught me valuable lessons and empowered me to create more than I imagined possible.

The Author

Michele Attias originates from Gibraltar and her professional career covers over 20 years in Personal Development. Her desire has always been driven by a need to make a difference in people's lives.

She qualified as a Therapist and Clinical Supervisor in Mental Health Services where she worked for a number of years treating depressed, anxious, addicted and bereaved clients, whilst supervising over 60 Therapists and their client caseloads.

After undergoing significant changes in her personal life, she re-invented herself and became a Certified Coach, Public Speaker and Writer, contributing articles to online platforms such as *Lifehack, Medium, Inbound, Divorced Moms* and *Personal Growth*. In 2014 she was nominated for the Women Inspiring Women Awards, and in 2017 was a Best Coach finalist in the Best Business Women Awards in the UK.

Michele coaches a diverse range of international professionals, corporates, lawyers, journalists, bankers, entrepreneurs, writers, managers, coaches, business owners and leaders. She is an expert at helping clients self-assess, gain clarity, and make productive decisions, even in the midst of uncertainty. Her skills come from an ability to listen, reframe thinking and empower clients to be comfortable with making decisions from a base of tranquil thought. With a huge knowledge of personal development, she cares deeply about people, combining these qualities with a no-nonsense approach to getting results.

To access Michele's coaching resources, audios, e-books and videos, or to request a coaching consultation, please go to her website www.micheleattiascoaching.com

- www.linkedin.com/in/micheleattiascoaching
- www.twitter.com/AttiasMichele
- www.instagram.com/micheleattias1
- www.facebook.com/AttiasMichele

24086645R00105

Printed in Poland
by Amazon Fulfillment
Poland Sp. z o.o., Wrocław